Word Processing
with Word

Learning Made Simple

Keith Brindley

Routledge
Taylor & Francis Group

LONDON AND NEW YORK

First published by Butterworth-Heinemann
This edition published 2011 by Routledge
2 Park Square, Milton Park, Abingdon, Oxon OX14 4RN
711 Third Avenue, New York, NY 10017, USA

Routledge is an imprint of the Taylor & Francis Group, an informa business

First edition 2006

Notice
No responsibility is assumed by the publisher for any injury
and/or damage to persons or property as a matter of products liability, negligence or otherwise, or from any use or
operation of any methods, products, instructions or ideas
contained in the material herein.

TRADEMARKS/REGISTERED TRADEMARKS
Computer hardware and software brand names mentioned in
this book are protected by their respective trademarks and are
acknowledged

British Library Cataloguing in Publication Data
A catalogue record for this book is available from the British
Library

ISBN-13: 978 0 7506 8187 2
ISBN-10: 0 7506 8187 X

 Typeset by Co-publications, Loughborough

Icons designed by Sarah Ward © 1994

Transferred to Digital Print 2011

Contents

Preface

The books in the Learning Made Simple series aim to do exactly what it says on the cover — make learning simple.

A Learning Made Simple book:

❏ Is **fully illustrated**: with clearly labelled screenshots.

❏ Is **easy to read**: with brief explanations, and clear instructions.

❏ Is **task-based**: each short section concentrates on one job at a time.

❏ **Builds knowledge**: ideas and techniques are presented in the right order so that your understanding builds progressively as you work through the book.

❏ **Is flexible**: as each section is self-contained, if you know it, you can skip it.

The books in the Learning Made Simple books series are designed with learning in mind, and so do not directly follow the structure of any specific syllabus — but they do cover the content. This book covers Module 3 of the ECDL syllabus and the Integrated e-Document Production aspects of New CLAIT. For details of how the sections map against your syllabus, please go to the website:

http://www.madesimple.co.uk

1　The basics

Starting up

First operation you ever do when using Word is to start it up. Use the ⏣ start button, and access its sub-menu.

3 Point to and click **Microsoft Word**

2 Point to the **All Programs** menu entry (you don't need to click)

Basic steps

1 Click the ⏣ start button

2 Point to the **All Programs** menu entry — a sub-menu entry pops out

3 Point to then click the **Microsoft Word** sub-menu entry (if you have Microsoft Office installed on your computer, you'll first have to point to the **MSOffice** sub-menu entry — which will create a further pop-out menu to locate the **Microsoft Word** sub-menu entry)

After starting, you will be presented with the main Word window (shown opposite). If your copy of Word has been adapted by any other user since installation, your screen may display something a little different.

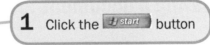

1 Click the ⏣ start button

Take note

This whole process of clicking the ⏣ start button (or a menu) and navigating to your required sub-menu entry is abbreviated from now on in this book as a statement such as:

choose **Start↦Microsoft Word**,

or:

choose **Tools↦Word Count**

2

Main features of a Word document window are shown below, but don't panic — they'll be looked at shortly. Soon you'll think Word is one of the easiest computer programs to get the hang of — and you'll be right.

The Word menu bar leads to commands available

Toolbars feature easily-clickable buttons which allow you to choose commands quickly

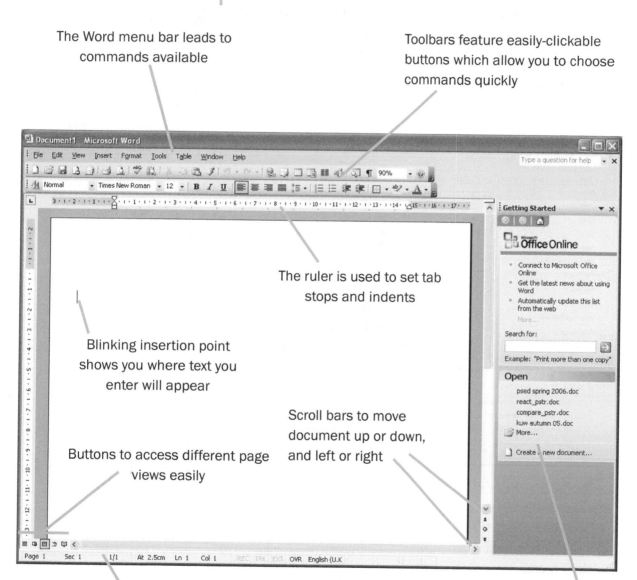

The ruler is used to set tab stops and indents

Blinking insertion point shows you where text you enter will appear

Scroll bars to move document up or down, and left or right

Buttons to access different page views easily

The status bar along the bottom gives details about the document in the window (see page 27 for more details)

The Task Pane — common tasks you may need to do in Word are listed here for you to use

Word menus

Word has nine menus in its menu bar. They hold all the commands and tools available to any user of Word. While you don't (and that's just as well!) need to know what *all* these commands and tools are to get good results from Word, it's worth looking at all the menus to get an overall feel for what they are about — use this page as a reference.

The menu bar itself looks like this:

Basic steps

1 To display a menu, click on its name in the menu bar

2 Alternatively, press [Alt]+ the menu's underlined letter

3 To remove a displayed menu, click anywhere else in the window

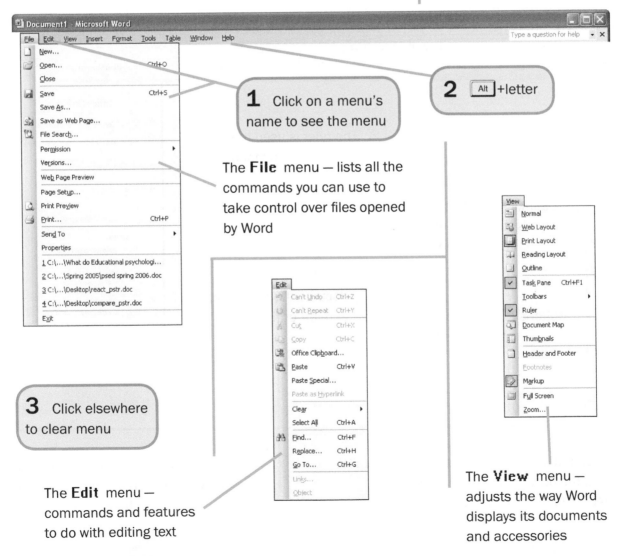

1 Click on a menu's name to see the menu

2 [Alt]+letter

The **File** menu — lists all the commands you can use to take control over files opened by Word

3 Click elsewhere to clear menu

The **Edit** menu — commands and features to do with editing text

The **View** menu — adjusts the way Word displays its documents and accessories

4

The **Insert** menu — used to place
certain features over and above
ordinary text into a document

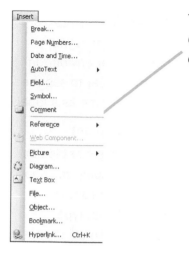

The **Tools** menu — special
features and controls

The **Table** menu — controls
aspects of tables within a
document

The **Format** menu — the
menu you use to apply styles
and so on to your document

The **Window** menu —
choose between documents
and control how they are
displayed

The **Help** menu — how to how
to?

Help me, I'm drowning!

Inevitably you will find there are times you don't know what you are doing. This happens whenever you are new (and, sometimes not-so-new) to a complex program like Word. Fortunately, Word has an incredibly useful — and even-more-incredibly comprehensive — help system built-in to it. This comes in three parts:

❐ first there are ScreenTips — little labels which show up (1) when you point over any of the myriads of buttons Word has in its many toolbars, and (2) at other specific places

❐ second is the Office Assistant — a sort of electronic dogs-body that monitors where you are within Word, and gives contextual help and advice if you need

❐ third is Help — an easily accessible system in which you can locate help about any feature, command or topic in Word.

Basic steps

■ **ScreenTips**

1 Simply position your pointer over any button in any toolbar to see the button's name as a label

■ **Office Assistant**

2 If Office Assistant is not already displayed, choose **Help⤳Microsoft Word Help**, type [Alt]+[H] then [H], or (best) type [F1]. Once displayed, as you move around within Word, the Office Assistant provides help

3 Type in a word or phrase describing what you'd like help about

> **1** ScreenTips give each button a name as the pointer passes over it

Numbering

What would you like to do?

Type your question here and then click Search.

Options   Search

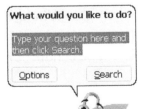

> **2** The Office Assistant — always there to lend a (slightly tacky) hand

Take note

If you find that help features are more a hindrance than a help, just turn them off. For example, turn off ScreenTips by unchecking the **Show ScreenTips on tool-bars** check box on the **Options** tab of the **Customize** dialog box (see page 11)

4 Click **Search**, or type <kbd>Alt</kbd> + <kbd>F</kbd>

5 In the resultant list of topics the Office Assistant displays about your request, click the one you want

6 The **Word Help** window is displayed, giving help about the topic you selected. Any sub-topics are listed for you to select further. Important terms are shown coloured for you to select, and any tips for the topic you asked for are shown. Click the sub-topic, term, or tip you want

Tip

You can also type in the thing you want help on, in the Ask a Question text box, on Word's menu bar. Press <kbd>↵</kbd> when you've done this and topics are listed for you to select

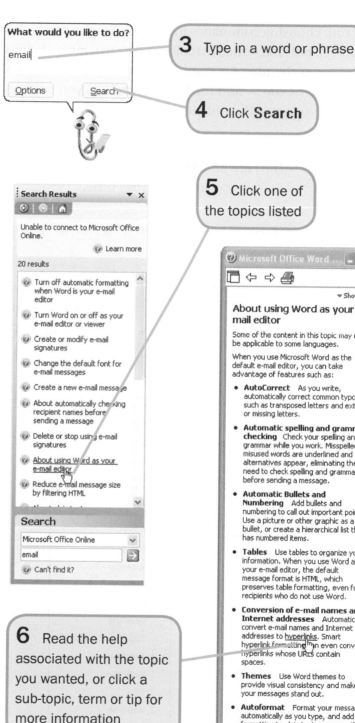

3 Type in a word or phrase

4 Click **Search**

5 Click one of the topics listed

6 Read the help associated with the topic you wanted, or click a sub-topic, term or tip for more information

7

Toolbars

Apart from choosing commands in menus, Word is controlled by on-screen buttons, found in toolbars. The two most obvious toolbars are at the top of a Word document but, as we'll see, there are others, too — and further — Word lets you customize them to your heart's content.

Basic steps

1 To display any particular toolbar, choose **View⤳Toolbars**

2 In the **Toolbars** pop-out menu, move to the toolbar you want displayed, then click

The Formatting toolbar — buttons used for common everyday tasks

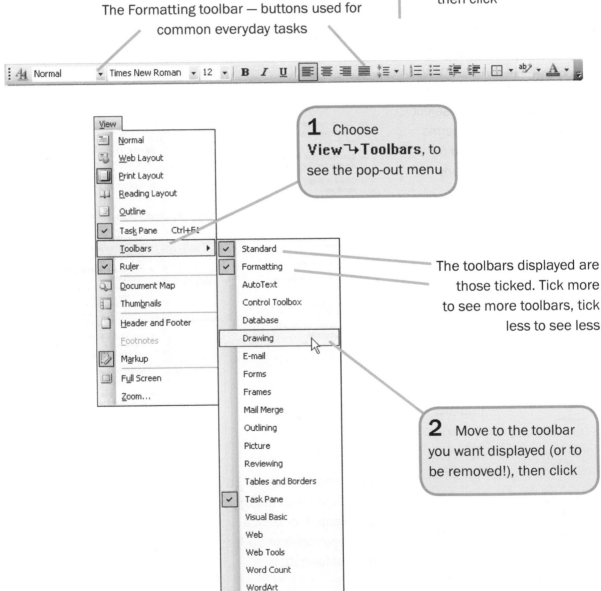

1 Choose **View⤳Toolbars**, to see the pop-out menu

The toolbars displayed are those ticked. Tick more to see more toolbars, tick less to see less

2 Move to the toolbar you want displayed (or to be removed!), then click

3 Alternatively, use the mouse shortcut — click any toolbar with the right mouse button

4 Click the toolbar you want turned on or off

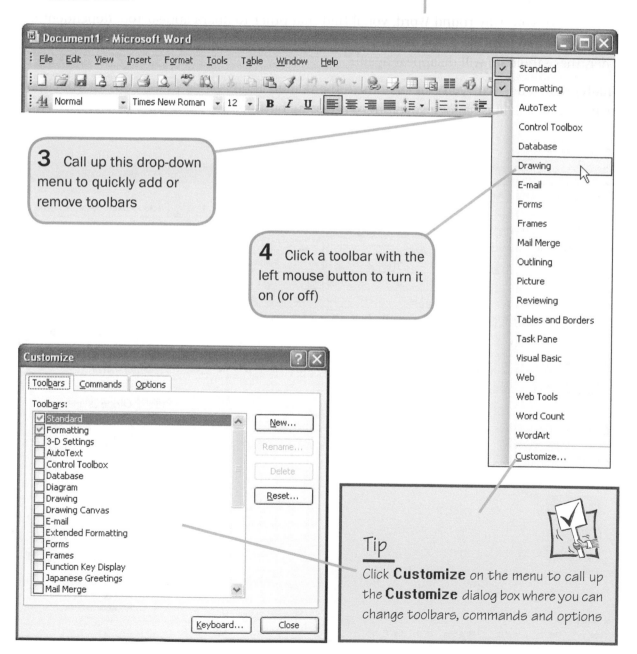

3 Call up this drop-down menu to quickly add or remove toolbars

4 Click a toolbar with the left mouse button to turn it on (or off)

Tip

Click **Customize** on the menu to call up the **Customize** dialog box where you can change toolbars, commands and options

Other toolbars

All default toolbars in Word are displayed below. While most appear initially fixed in position in the document window, you can move many of them by dragging them away from their initial positions — at which point they become floating toolbars, movable anywhere you might have some screen space suitable. Any new toolbars you create for yourself float too.

As you work your way round Word, you'll find that other toolbars appear too, dependent on what you are attempting to do. When you have finished that particular task, or switch to another, these toolbars will disappear again.

Finally, remember that you can customize the default toolbars, as well as any of your own creations, by moving, removing, adding, or creating buttons.

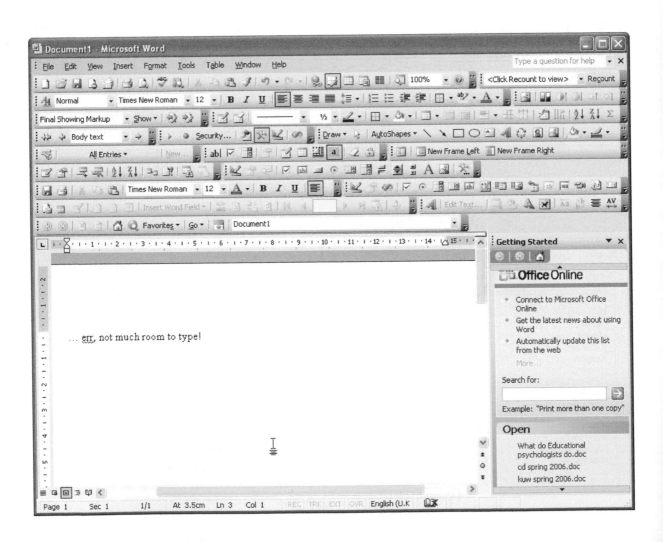

Buttons

Buttons on toolbars are graphically representative of their function. As a result it's easy to see what most of them do. However, some buttons are a little more obscure. Here the standard and formatting toolbar buttons are listed together with brief explanations.

Take note

There are many, many more buttons hidden within Word's interface, either pre-formatted onto other toolbars, or unused in a default installation. There's nothing to stop you using or customizing these, or even creating your own buttons from scratch

- — new document
- — open document
- — save document
- — permission
- — e-mail
- — print document
- — print preview
- — spelling and grammar
- — research
- — cut
- — copy
- — paste
- — format painter
- — undo

- — redo
- — insert hyperlink
- — tables and borders
- — insert table
- — insert Excel worksheet
- — columns
- — drawing
- — document map
- ¶ — show/hide ¶
- 90% — zoom control
- — help
- — styles and formatting
- Normal — style
- Times New Roman — font
- 12 — font size

- **B** — bold
- *I* — italic
- U — underline
- — align left
- — align centre
- — align right
- — justify
- — numbering
- — bullets
- — decrease indent
- — increase indent
- — borders
- — highlight
- A — font colour

Views in Word

Word allows a number of different views of your document — normal view, for example, is simply the one new documents often default to. It's important to remember, though, that each view of a document makes absolutely no difference to what's actually in the document — it's just one way of looking at it on your computer screen. Very often, the view you might choose depends on what you are actually using Word for.

1 Your document is probably already in normal view (see below). If not, choose **View → Normal**, or type Alt + V then N, or (best) click the Normal view button ≣ at the bottom left of your document window

1 Normal view

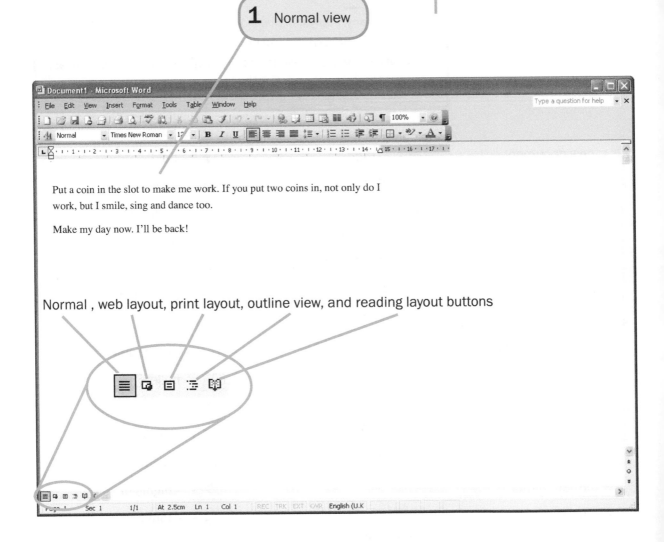

Normal , web layout, print layout, outline view, and reading layout buttons

Print layout view

2 Choose **View→Print Layout**, or type Alt + V then P, or (best) click the Print layout button at the bottom left of your document window

cont...

Another important view of your documents is provided by print layout view. As its name infers, print layout view lets you see how the printed page will appear — *what you see is what you get* (WYSIWYG). Margins and borders around text are shown, as well as positions of graphics. This is a useful view to check the final appearance of your document before printing.

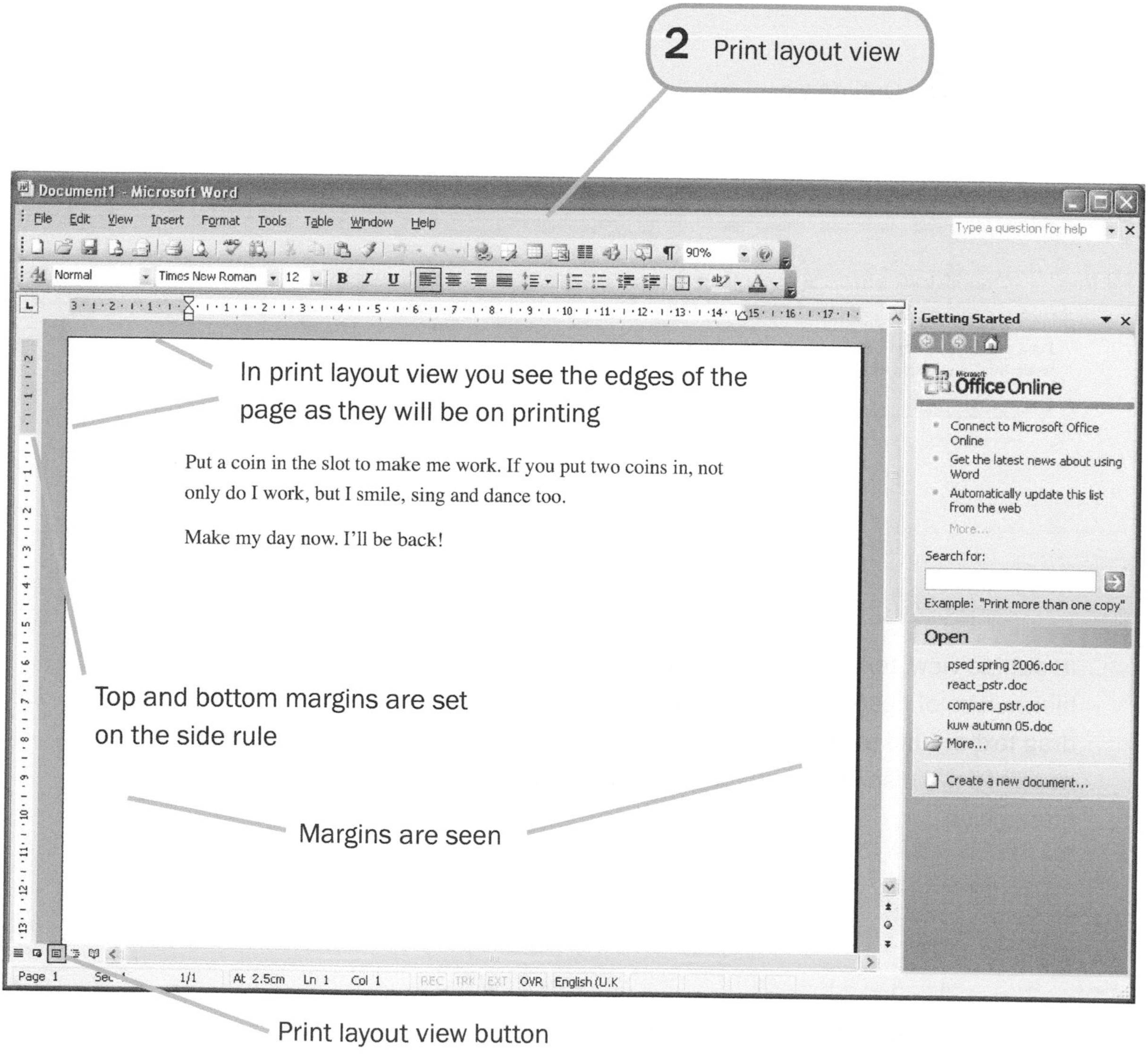

2 Print layout view
Document1 - Microsoft Word
In print layout view you see the edges of the page as they will be on printing
Put a coin in the slot to make me work. If you put two coins in, not only do I work, but I smile, sing and dance too.
Make my day now. I'll be back!
Top and bottom margins are set on the side rule
Margins are seen
Getting Started
Office Online
Print layout view button

Outline view

The final important view of Word documents we'll consider here is outline view. Outline view allows you to control how the various levels of heading and subheadings in your document are displayed (or not displayed) and organized. It's the ideal method of rearranging documents by moving complete blocks of text long distances within the document, or changing the hierarchy of headings.

3 To show your documents in outline view, choose **View→Outline**, or type ⌐Alt⌐+⌐V⌐ then ⌐O⌐, or (best) click the Outline view button ▤ at the bottom left of your document window

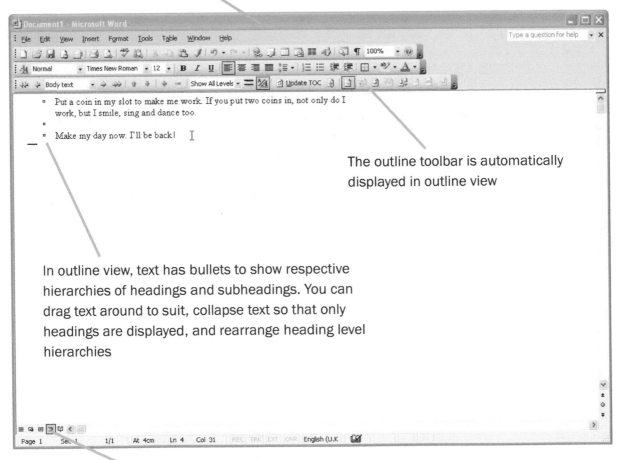

3 Outline view

The outline toolbar is automatically displayed in outline view

In outline view, text has bullets to show respective hierarchies of headings and subheadings. You can drag text around to suit, collapse text so that only headings are displayed, and rearrange heading level hierarchies

The outline view button

Zooming

Basic steps

1 Click the down arrow of the zoom control button of the standard toolbar

2 From the resultant drop-down menu, choose your desired zoom percentage

3 As an alternative you can choose **View → Zoom**, to call up the **Zoom** dialog box, and select zoom value there

You can magnify or reduce part of a document page in Word, to get a close up or overall view of the page or part of it. This is known as zooming.

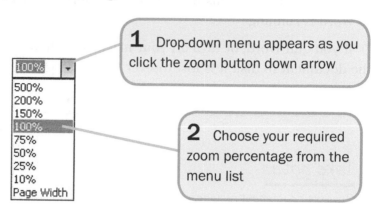

1 Drop-down menu appears as you click the zoom button down arrow

2 Choose your required zoom percentage from the menu list

Choose your zoom percentage here

3 The **Zoom** dialog box

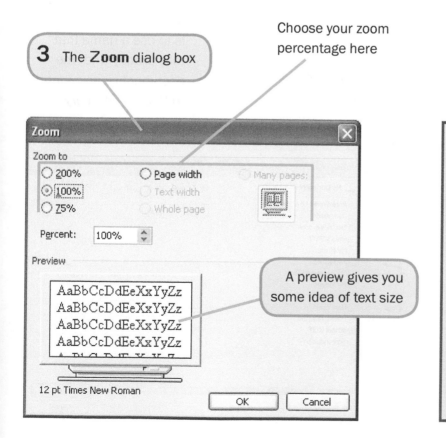

A preview gives you some idea of text size

Tip

You can also change your zoom view by selecting (either by double-clicking or dragging across) the percentage value in the zoom button box — or the zoom percent box of the Zoom dialog box — and typing in your required zoom value, before finally pressing ⏎

Saving a document

Once you've worked on a document you need to save it onto disk because:

❐ the document remains in computer memory only as long as Word is running

❐ if you quit Word, or turn off your machine without saving the document to disk it is lost forever — **RIP**

> ## Take note
>
> Save your document regularly, throughout working on it. That way, if your machine buckaroos — or you do something silly — your work is not lost — at least up to the last save operation

1 The **Save As** dialog box

2 Enter a document name here, or use the suggested default (which is the first line of your document)

Basic steps

1 Choose **File⤷Save**, or type **Alt**+**F** then **S**, or type **Ctrl**+**S**, or click the Save button 💾, to call the **Save As** dialog box if this is the first time you have saved the document. If you have already saved the document the **Save As** dialog box isn't even called up — the document is simply saved over itself with the same file name

2 Enter a name in the **File name** box — a good idea is to use a name that tells exactly what the document is, say — *letter to Bob 30 February*

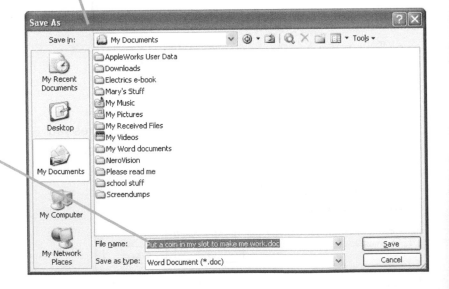

3 Click the folder you want to save the document in

4 Click **Open** to open the folder

5 Click **Save** to save the document

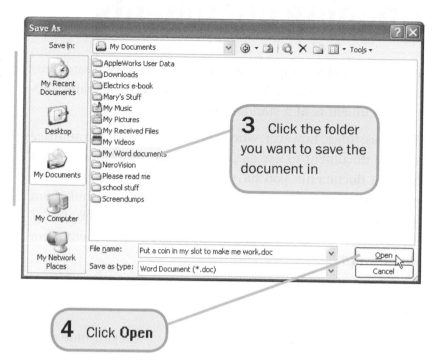

3 Click the folder you want to save the document in

4 Click **Open**

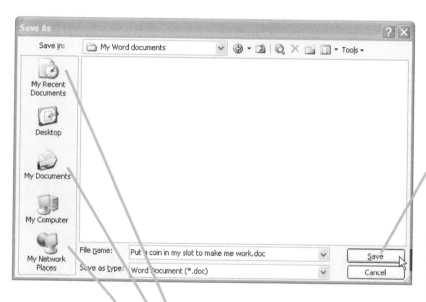

5 Click **Save**

To locate other folders, or other places, to store your Word document, you can use these buttons in the **Save As** dialog box

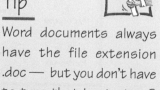

Tip

Word documents always have the file extension .doc — but you don't have to type that in at step 2 — Word does it for you automatically

Opening documents

When you first startup Word a new document is created automatically for you, ready for you to enter text. Usually, this new document is of a standard form.

There are times, however, when you may need to open another style of document to use as your new one, or even just open existing documents you have previously saved. If you have worked on these documents recently, you might find them listed in the Documents folder of the ⊞start menu, but if it's been a while since using them, you can open them from within Word.

Basic steps

1 Choose **File→Open,** or type Alt+F then O, or type Ctrl+O, or click the Open button 📂. The **Open** dialog box is shown

2 Locate the folder that contains the document you wish to open

3 Click **Open**

1 **Open** dialog box

Clicking here allows you to choose to view a preview of documents — see Tip bottom-right

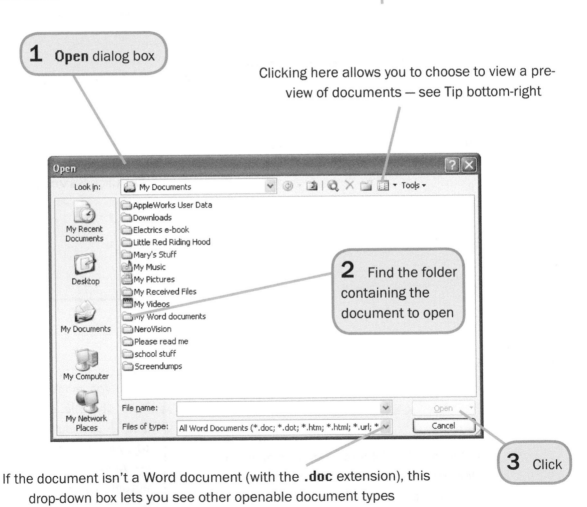

2 Find the folder containing the document to open

3 Click

If the document isn't a Word document (with the **.doc** extension), this drop-down box lets you see other openable document types

4 In the folder, select the document you want to open

5 Click **Open**

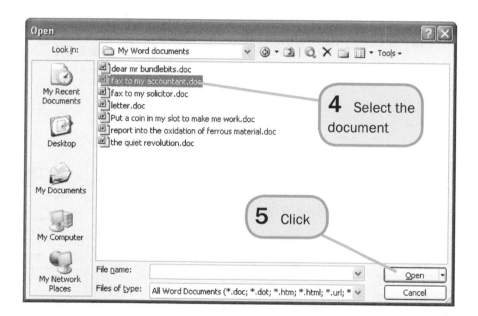

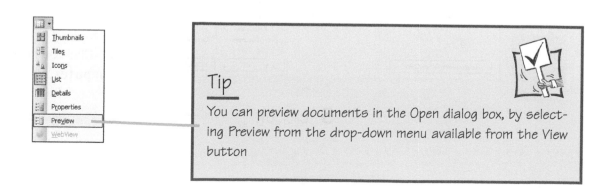

Creating new documents

Creating a new document is just as easy as opening an existing document. Word creates a new document as the image of a template. Templates are ready-built and installed document *plans*, complete with styles (see page 102) and formats you might want to use for any particular appearance of document (see page 112 for further details of templates).

Templates are arranged in sections, accessed in the Template dialog box with tabs.

(see page 102)
(see page 112 for further details of templates)

Basic steps

1 Choose **File⤷New**. The **New Document** Task Pane is displayed

2 Click **On my computer...**

3 In the **Templates** dialog box, click a tab of the document type you want to create

4 Select a template

5 Click **OK**

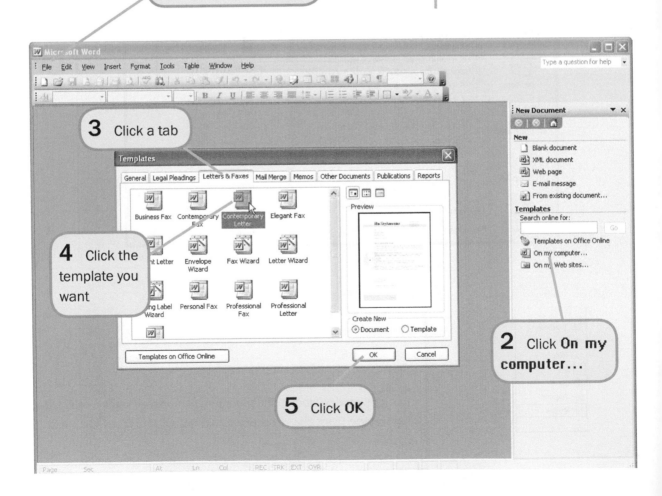

1 Choose **File⤷New**

3 Click a tab

4 Click the template you want

5 Click **OK**

2 Click **On my computer...**

Basic steps

1 On the desktop, locate the folder holding the Word document you want to create a new copy from

2 Click the document with the right mouse button

3 In the shortcut menu, click **New** with your left mouse button — a copy of the document is opened

Creating new from old

You can create new documents from other documents, too.

If you have, say, a letter (or any other type of Word document) that you have previously written, and decide that it is in the same or similar format as another you want to send, you can simply open the existing document and change the details you need to change, saving considerable time.

Tip

This works even when you don't have Word running. When you create the new document at step 3, Word is automatically launched

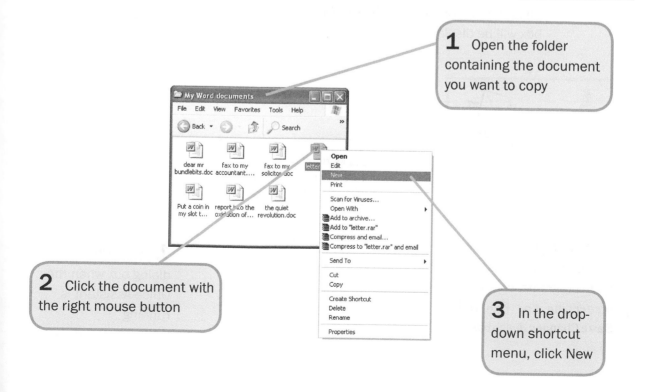

1 Open the folder containing the document you want to copy

2 Click the document with the right mouse button

3 In the drop-down shortcut menu, click New

Goodbye — or au revoir?

After you've finished using a computer program it's usual to exit or quit it. If you're only trying to clear the screen for a short while, on the other hand, there are alternatives.

Basic steps

- **Quitting or exiting Word**

1 Choose **File➔Exit**, or type `Alt`+`F` then `X`. If you have recently saved the documents you are working on and have not worked on them since, Word quits straightaway. If you have worked on a document since last saving it (or have not saved it at all) the **Save Changes** dialog box is displayed. This varies depending on whether you have the Office Assistant running or not

2 If you have not saved the document recently, click **Yes**

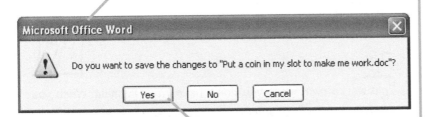

1 **Save Changes** dialog box when the Office Assistant is not running

Microsoft Office Word

⚠ Do you want to save the changes to "Put a coin in my slot to make me work.doc"?

[Yes] [No] [Cancel]

2 Click to save. If you have not saved the document before this, the **Save As** dialog box will be displayed (see page 16)

Tip

You don't actually have to quit programs before you shut down your computer. Just choose **start** **➔Shut Down**, and the computer exits all your open programs correctly, presenting the required **Save Changes** dialog boxes to suit

⚠ **Microsoft Office Word**

Do you want to save the changes to "Put a coin in my slot to make me work.doc"?

[Yes] [No] [Cancel]

1 Save Changes dialog box when the Office Assistant is running

Temporarily clearing your screen

■ **Minimizing Word**

1 Click a window's **Mini-mize** button , at the top right corner

2 Click the window's button on the Taskbar, to restore the window

If you're only trying to clear your screen for a short while — and you don't want to quit Word — click the Minimize button  at the top-right of the Word program window. This minimizes the program window as a button on the taskbar — showing the document name (as long as it's not too long).

1 Click the **Minimize** button here

Take note

While the technique here works for a Word program window, it doesn't work for individual document windows. Some previous versions of Word allowed you to minimize individual document windows within the program window as well as the complete program window, but recent versions of Word only allow you to minimize the complete program window.

While minimizing windows can be confusing for a new user, used properly it can help clear up your Desktop. However, it's best to remember that programs should not be left long term in this mode — exiting them correctly as shown opposite clears up computer memory for other tasks

Hovering the cursor over a taskbar button produces a screentip, displaying the document name and program

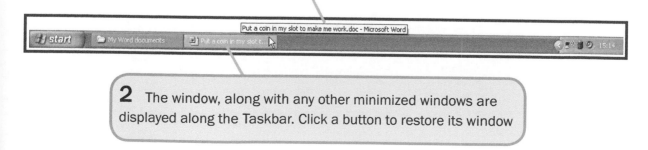

Put a coin in my slot to make me work.doc - Microsoft Word

start | My Word documents | Put a coin in my slot t. | 15:14

2 The window, along with any other minimized windows are displayed along the Taskbar. Click a button to restore its window

Exercises

1   Start up Word

2   Type a few lines of text into the blank Word document

3   Change the zoom percentage of the document to 150%

4   Save the document on the Desktop, and close it

5   Open the document again in Word

6   View the document in print layout view

7   Display the Word Count toolbar

8   Create a new document using the Contemporary Letter template

9   Create a new document, based on the one you saved at Exercise 4

10   Minimize all documents

2 Text essentials

Entering text

As a word processor, of course, Word's main function is to store straightforward text. As you startup Word, or create a new document, you can begin to enter text immediately.

Basic steps

1 Simply type something. It doesn't matter what — a few lines of rubbish will do nicely

2 If your document is important, remember to save it

1 Enter text into document

2 Click the save button 🖫 to save your document

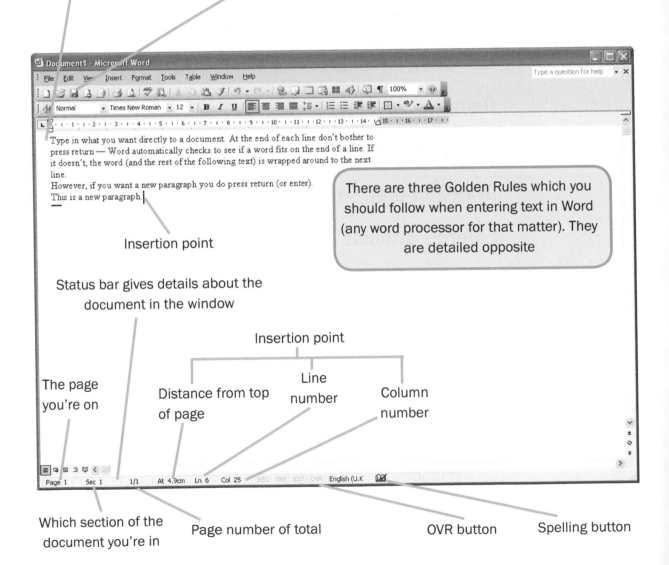

Type in what you want directly to a document. At the end of each line don't bother to press return — Word automatically checks to see if a word fits on the end of a line. If it doesn't, the word (and the rest of the following text) is wrapped around to the next line.
However, if you want a new paragraph you do press return (or enter).
This is a new paragraph.

There are three Golden Rules which you should follow when entering text in Word (any word processor for that matter). They are detailed opposite

Insertion point

Status bar gives details about the document in the window

Insertion point

The page you're on

Distance from top of page

Line number

Column number

Which section of the document you're in

Page number of total

OVR button

Spelling button

26

The status bar

Get into the habit of looking at the status bar. It gives some explicit information about what's happening within your Word document, such as:

- page number, section (you can break your document up into smaller sections, to make it more manageable — see page 68) number, and total number of pages

- location of the insertion point (that is, the point within text where your keyboard entries appear on screen)

- overtype button — active when blacked (that is, not greyed). See over for details

- spelling button — if the button displays an ✗ mark, Word has detected a spelling error

Take note

The Golden Rules of Word

1   Never, never, never, never, never, never, never, never, never, never (get the message?) put two spaces together. The old typists' routine of putting two spaces at the end of a sentence should not be done in a word processor because spaces aren't generally of a fixed width. A program like Word adjusts spaces to ensure the text fits its given column width and looks good. Two or more spaces together may be adjusted in width to give ridiculously wide spaces between words. For the same reason, text which is formed into tabular columns mustn't be created by inserting spaces to line columns up — it might look aligned on screen, but when it prints you can't guarantee it — use proper tabs instead (see page 58)

2   Never, never, never, never (oh, here we go again) put two carriage returns together. Actually, this isn't quite so critical as Golden Rule number 1, but important nevertheless. Spaces between paragraphs are best controlled by creating styles for each paragraph type (see page 102) which incorporate spaces before and after them

3   Never (once is enough this time, I'm sure) press ⏎ or `Enter` at the end of a line of text — unless the end of the line is also the end of a paragraph. There is simply no need — and carriage returns fix the text to those line lengths. Use Word's word-wrapping facility to do it automatically — then any later changes will adjust automatically

Editing text

Inevitably you will make mistakes in your work. This is where a word processor like Word shows its forte — mistakes can be edited on-screen before printing. Even if a mistake slips by you, and you only see it after printing, you can correct it and reprint the document.

Even if your required corrections aren't due to mistakes, but are straightforward editorial changes, Word has some unbeatable facilities for making any kind of textual change necessary in a document.

There are several ways you can edit text. The simplest — covered here — is overtyping.

Deleting, changing and inserting text, on the other hand, rely on the principle of placing the insertion point at the point which requires editing! If you learn nothing else from this page, learn this fact.

- **Overtype editing**

1 If you spot a mistake which requires you to re-type part or all of a word or sentence, position the insertion point at the beginning of the mistake

2 Look at the overtype button OVR on the status bar. If it is greyed, you are in insert edit mode, if it is black you are in overtype edit mode. Double-click it to toggle between the two modes. Make sure you are in overtype edit mode (the button should be in blackface (ie OVR)

1 As you move the mouse pointer over text it changes to the I-beam pointer I. When you position the pointer over the point to edit then click, the insertion point of Word becomes active at that point. This whole process of pointing and clicking with the I-beam pointer I is known as positioning the insertion point.

Remember it — because all editing relies on it!

There was a cow stupefied on a hill. If it hasn't gonn it will be their still. Now is the time for all good men to come to the aid of the party

3 Retype the section of text — this overtypes text already there

4 Move to any other areas you need to overtype as in Step 1

5 When you have finished overtyping, double-click the overtype button OVR again, to return to insertion mode

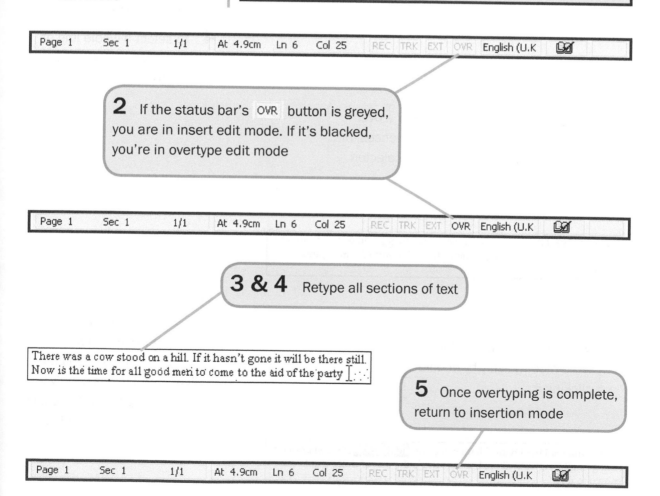

| Page 1 | Sec 1 | 1/1 | At 4.9cm | Ln 6 | Col 25 | REC | TRK | EXT | OVR | English (U.K |

2 If the status bar's OVR button is greyed, you are in insert edit mode. If it's blacked, you're in overtype edit mode

| Page 1 | Sec 1 | 1/1 | At 4.9cm | Ln 6 | Col 25 | REC | TRK | EXT | OVR | English (U.K |

3 & 4 Retype all sections of text

There was a cow stood on a hill. If it hasn't gone it will be there still. Now is the time for all good men to come to the aid of the party

5 Once overtyping is complete, return to insertion mode

| Page 1 | Sec 1 | 1/1 | At 4.9cm | Ln 6 | Col 25 | REC | TRK | EXT | OVR | English (U.K |

Selecting text

Whenever you want to edit text (that is, apart from when you overtype — see previous page) you need to select the particular text you want to change. Word allows you to do this in various ways. No single way is best: instead, a combination of selecting techniques — depending on what is to be selected — should be used.

Selection of text is sometimes known by different names such as blocking or highlighting. These names are often merely descriptive of the selection process — text which is selected becomes highlighted or blocked and that's how you know the text happens to be selected!

Basic steps

1 You can select any letter, word, sentence, paragraph, or any part of these by dragging over the required text

2 To select a single word, double-click it

3 To select more than one word, drag from one word across to the next, or further if you want more words to be selected

4 To select a whole line of text, click in the selection bar to the left of the line

cont...

1 Drag the I-beam pointer I over the letters, or words, or sentences, or paragraphs you want to be selected

No, no, no, said the Giant. There can be no suggestion of a compromise. I am going to eat you all up, because that's the sort of thing giants are known to do.

2 You can select a single word most quickly by double-clicking it

As you drag over your selected text and release the mouse button, the selected text becomes highlighted. Highlighted text is simply the visible sign that the text is selected

No, no, no, said the Giant. There can be no suggsetion of a compromise. I am going to eat you all up, because that's the sort of thing giants are known to do.

3 Drag over words to select them. As you drag over each new part of a word the whole word becomes selected automatically

No, no, no, said the Giant. There can be no suggsetion of a compromise. I am going to eat you all up; **because that's the** sort of thing giants are known to do.

Tip

When you begin selecting in the middle of a word, then drag to include part of another word, Word automatically selects both words (and any subsequent ones too), as well as any space after the words

4 Select whole lines of text by clicking in the selection bar

 No, no, no, said the Giant. There can be no suggsetion of a compromise. I am going to eat you all up, because that's the sort of thing giants are known to do.

The selection bar is to the left of text on any Word document page

Take note

All of these selection techniques can be used to select graphic items, such as pictures, as well as text

Selecting text (cont)

No, no, no, said the Giant. There can be no suggsetion of a compromise. I am going to eat you all up, because that's the sort of thing giants are known to do.

5 Select multiple lines of text by dragging in the selection bar

6 Select a single sentence by holding down Ctrl and clicking in the sentence

No, no, no, said the Giant. There can be no suggsetion of a compromise. I am going to eat you all up, because that's the sort of thing giants are known to do.

7 Double-click in the selection bar (or triple-click in the text) to select a paragraph

No, no, no, said the Giant. There can be no suggsetion of a compromise. I am going to eat you all up, because that's the sort of thing giants are known to do.

8 Drag across paragraphs in the selection bar to select multiple paragraphs

No, no, no, said the Giant. There can be no suggsetion of a compromise. I am going to eat you all up, because that's the sort of thing giants are known to do.
With that he picked up Jack and lifted him towards his mouth. Once inside the Giant's mouth Jack realised his time was nigh unless he did some quick thinking. He decided to go for broke and tickled the Giant's tonsils.

5 To select multiple lines of text, drag in the selection bar to the left of the lines

6 To select a sentence, hold down Ctrl and click anywhere in the sentence

7 To select a paragraph, either double-click in the selection bar to the left of the paragraph, or triple-click anywhere in the text

8 To select multiple paragraphs, drag in the selection bar to the left of the paragraphs

9 To select an entire document, triple-click in the selection bar

10 To select text which is neither a whole word, sentence, or paragraph, position the insertion point at the beginning of the text, then hold down Shift and click at the end of the text

Take two aspirins and call me in the mroning. The dogs sat on the mat.
When the Queen of Hearts had no tea the Knave of Hearts stole the tarts.
Instead she beat the Knave of Hearts soundly and sent him to bed.

No, no, no, said the Giant. There can be no suggsetion of a compromise.
I am going to eat you all up, because that's the sort of thing giants are
known to do.

With that he picked up Jack and lifted him towards his mouth. Once
inside the Giant's mouth Jack realised his time was nigh unless he did
some quick thinking. He decided to go for broke and tickled the Giant's
tonsils.

Tip

Cancel a selection by clicking outside it, or pressing any arrow key

9 Select entire document by triple-clicking

No, no, no, said the Giant. There can be no suggsetion of a compromise.
I am going to eat you all up, because that's the sort of thing giants are
known to do.

With that he picked up Jack and lifted him towards his mouth. Once
inside the Giant's mouth Jack realised his time was nigh unless he did
some quick thinking. He decided to go for broke and tickled the Giant's
tonsils.

Keyboard shortcuts

You can select text with the keyboard too:

One character right	Shift + →
One character left	Shift + ←
To the end of a word	Ctrl + Shift + →
To the beginning of a word	Ctrl + Shift + ←
To the end of a line	Shift + End
To the beginning of a line	Shift + Home
One line down	Shift + ↓
One line up	Shift + ↑
To the end of a paragraph	Ctrl + Shift + ↓
To the start of a paragraph	Ctrl + Shift + ↑
One screen down	Shift + Page Down
One screen up	Shift + Page Up
To end of document	Ctrl + Shift + End
To beginning of document	Ctrl + Shift + Home
Entire document	Ctrl + A

10 Click at the starting point, then hold down Shift and click at the finishing point, to select a complete block of text

Tip

Remember that no single selection method is best for all purposes. Learn all the methods, then choose which one suits at any time

Ooops — a mistake!

Word processors are meant to make the correction of mistakes as simple as possible. Apart from the proper editing facilities of Word we've already seen, however, are extra goodies which make the correction of simple typing errors almost as easy as making the mistakes in the first place — but not qwite, if you see what I mean!

It's as well to know all these goodies to get the best out of Word. The mistakes we're concerned with here are those which you notice almost as you make them:

❐ obvious spelling errors

❐ mis-hit keys

❐ style changes which shouldn't have been made

and so on.

1 If you have just a few letters you want to delete, a quick result can be to press [←], or [delete]. Start by clicking the insertion point in place, then:

■ [←] deletes the character before the insertion point

■ [delete] deletes the character after the insertion point

■ [Ctrl]+[←] deletes the word before the insertion point

■ [Ctrl]+[delete] deletes the word after the insertion point

[←] deletes the character (in this case the space) before the insertion point

[delete] deletes the character after the insertion point

> No, no, no, no, no, said the Giant. There can be no suggsetion of a compromise. I am going to eat you all up, because that's the sort of thing giants are known to do.

[Ctrl]+[←] deletes the word before the insertion point — the word *no* in this case

1 Insertion point

[Ctrl]+[delete] deletes the word after the insertion point — *suggsetion* in this case

2 You can very often undo a mistake or change you make in a Word document, because Word features a multiple undo facility. Just click the Undo button 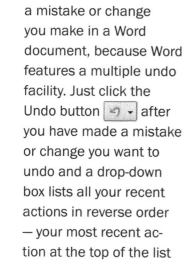 after you have made a mistake or change you want to undo and a drop-down box lists all your recent actions in reverse order — your most recent action at the top of the list

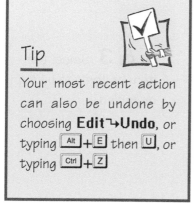

2 Clicking the Undo button displays a drop-down list box

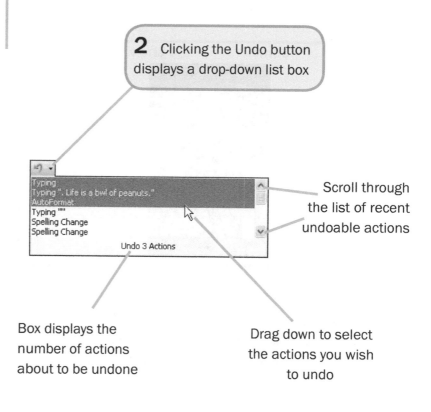

Typing
Typing ". Life is a bwl of peanuts."
AutoFormat
Typing ""
Spelling Change
Spelling Change

Undo 3 Actions

Scroll through the list of recent undoable actions

Box displays the number of actions about to be undone

Drag down to select the actions you wish to undo

Cut, copy and paste

Word (like any Windows application) uses a temporary storage area known as the Clipboard to keep items you want to move or copy within a Word document. These items can be of text or graphic forms (or a mixture of both). Using the Clipboard to do this is known as cutting, copying and pasting:

❐ you *cut* an item onto the Clipboard when you want to re-move it from one place in a document and move it to another place

❐ you *copy* an item onto the Clipboard when you want it to occur at more than one place in your document

❐ taking an item from the Clipboard and putting it in your document is known as *pasting.*

■ **Cutting**

1 Select the item or items you want to cut onto the Clipboard. This can be a selection of text, a graphi-cal item, or a combina-tion of the two

2 Choose **Edit↦Cut**, or type Alt+E then T, or type Ctrl+X, or simply click the Cut button to cut the selected item — it disappears from your Word document and is moved onto the Clipboard

---

Come and see the show

[image: photograph of a ferris wheel]

On the other hand, this is boring part of this document. Let's liven it up by moving the graphic image down here!

> **1 & 3** Select the item or items to be cut or copied

Use whichever selection method is appropriate for the text (or graphic in this case) to be copied or cut. To select this graphic, clicking in the selection bar is fastest

> **2 & 4** Cut or copy the item or items

> **5** Position the insertion point before pasting

Come and see the show

On the other hand, this is boring part of this document. Let's liven it up by moving the graphic image down here!

Copying

3 Select the item or items you want to copy

4 Choose **Edit↪Copy**, or type `Alt`+`E` then `C`, or type `Ctrl`+`C`, or click the Copy button `[⎘]` — the selection stays in your document but is copied onto the Clipboard too

Pasting

5 Position the insertion point where you want the item or items stored on the Clipboard to be pasted

6 Choose **Edit↪Paste**, or type `Alt`+`E` then `P`, or type `Ctrl`+`V`, or click the Paste button `[⎘]` to paste the item or items into your document

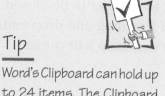

Tip

Word's Clipboard can hold up to 24 items. The Clipboard is shared with other Office programs, so items can be copied from one program and pasted into another

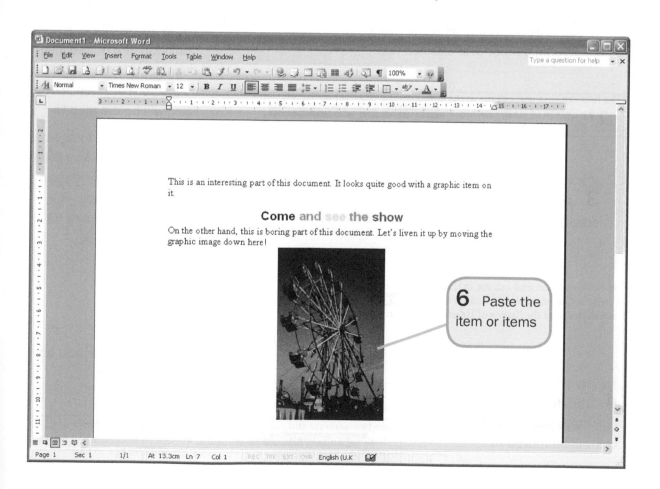

This is an interesting part of this document. It looks quite good with a graphic item on it.

Come and see the show

On the other hand, this is boring part of this document. Let's liven it up by moving the graphic image down here!

6 Paste the item or items

Drag-and-drop editing

Word has an extremely useful feature in its ability to allow selected text to be moved or copied by dragging. Proper use of this drag-and-drop editing can speed up incorporation of revisions in a document.

1 Select the text

> Take two aspirins and call me in the mroning. The dogs sat on the mat. When the Queen of Hearts had no tea the Knave of Hearts stole the tarts. Instead she beat the Knave of Hearts soundly and sent him to bed.

2 The arrow pointer replaces the I-beam pointer over selected text

> Take two aspirins and call me in the mroning. The dogs sat on the mat. When the Queen of Hearts had no tea the Knave of Hearts stole the tarts. Instead she beat the Knave of Hearts soundly and sent him to bed.

3 As you drag the selected text, the drag-and-drop pointer is displayed

> Take two aspirins and call me in the mroning. The dogs sat on the mat. When the Queen of Hearts had no tea the Knave of Hearts stole the tarts. Instead she beat the Knave of Hearts soundly and sent him to bed.

4 The dotted insertion point tells you where the text will be moved to

5 The text moves as you let go the mouse button

> Take two aspirins and call me in the mroning. The dogs sat on the mat. When the Knave of Hearts stole the tarts the Queen of Hearts had no tea. Instead she beat the Knave of Hearts soundly and sent him to bed.

■ **Moving selected text**

1 Select the text to be moved

2 Position the pointer over the selected text — the I-beam pointer ⌶ changes to the arrow pointer ⌖

3 Click on the selected text and drag the pointer — it changes to the drag-and-drop pointer

4 As you drag the drag-and-drop pointer to a new position, the dotted insertion point follows indicating where the selected text will be dragged to

5 When you have located the dotted insertion point where you want, release the mouse button. The selected text moves to the new location

Copying selected text

6 Select text as before

7 Drag the selected text as before

8 Locate the position you wish to copy text to as before (with the dotted insertion point)

9 Before you let go the mouse button, press and hold down `Ctrl` — the drag-and-drop pointer changes to show a plus symbol indicating Word is ready to copy (that is, not just move) text

10 Let go the mouse button to copy text to the new location

Tip

Drag-and-drop editing is really just an extension of the cut, copy and paste principle. As a result, you can drag-and-drop graphical items, or a combination of graphical and text items, as well as just text

---

No, **no, no,** said the Giant. There can be no suggsetion of a compromise. I am going to eat you all up, because that's the sort of thing giants are known to do.

6 Select text to be copied

7 Drag selected text with drag-and-drop pointer

No, **no, no,** said the Giant. There can be no suggsetion of a compromise. I am going to eat you all up, because that's the sort of thing giants are known to do.

8 Locate the dotted insertion point where you want the text to be copied to

No, **no, no,** said the Giant. There can be no suggsetion of a compromise. I am going to eat you all up, because that's the sort of thing giants are known to do.

9 Hold down `Ctrl` to copy selected text (indicated by + symbol on drag-and-drop pointer)

10 As you release the mouse button, selected text is copied

No, no, no, **no, no,** said the Giant. There can be no suggsetion of a compromise. I am going to eat you all up, because that's the sort of thing giants are known to do.

Entering symbols

Although Word is a word processor, very often it's necessary to include symbols within text. Examples of such symbols are:

❑ mathematical or scientific symbols — Ω μ ß ∝ for example (however, if you want to include complete mathematical formulae or expressions into your work it is best to use Word's integral equation editor, which is beyond the scope of this book)

❑ dingbats — the bullet (❑) at the left of this list is an example of a dingbat. Others are ✄ ☞ ♣ ● ♠ which can be used to embellish text

❑ typographical symbols and marks — the most obvious examples of typographical marks are the curly quotes (' and ") which differentiate properly typeset text from typewritten (with straight quotes — ' and ") text together with en dashes (–) and em dashes (—)

❑ foreign letters with accents — é ü å õ ç

and so on.

The ability to enter such symbols rapidly greatly enhances a word processor. Word has a special **Symbol** command which simplifies the task.

Basic steps

1 Position the insertion point where you want the symbol to be (if you are typing in text and want to enter the symbol as you go, the insertion point is already positioned correctly). Now choose **Insert↪Symbol**, or type `Alt`+`I` then `S`. This calls up the **Symbol** dialog box which automatically displays symbols available in fonts

2 Click a symbol and it is displayed enlarged. Click **Insert** if you want the symbol in your text. Alternatively, double-click the symbol. It is placed in text at the position of the insertion point

3 Display and choose different fonts with the **Font** drop-down list box

Tip

Use typographer's symbols and marks to give your work that professional edge. Automatically include curly quotes using Word's AutoCorrect feature (page 92). Use an en dash to combine number ranges (eg, pages 40–41) and use an em dash to separate emphasising text — just like that!

1 The **Symbol** dialog box

Click this tab to see any special characters that are included in any font (see below)

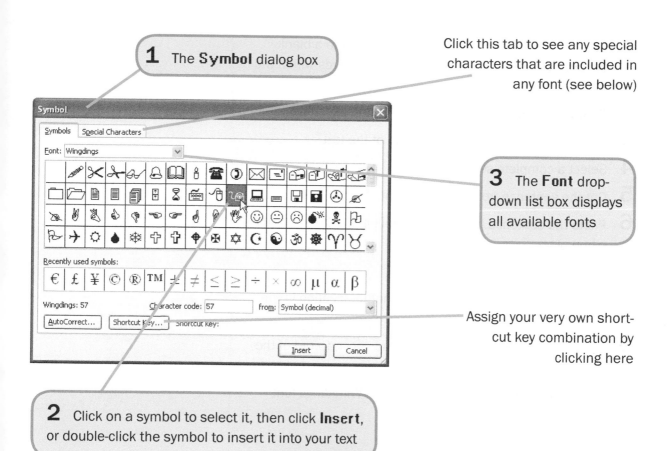

3 The **Font** drop-down list box displays all available fonts

Assign your very own short-cut key combination by clicking here

2 Click on a symbol to select it, then click **Insert**, or double-click the symbol to insert it into your text

Special characters are listed along with shortcut key combinations. Click on a character then click Insert (or simply double-click the character) to insert it into your text

Scroll through the list to see more characters

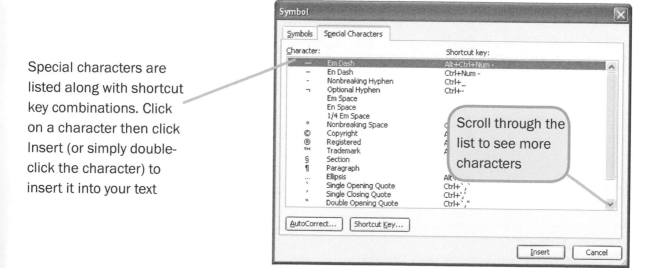

Exercises

1 Start up Word, and type a few lines of text into a blank document, then select three consecutive words within the text (any three will do)

2 Copy the three words

3 Paste the three words on to the end of the text

4 Select a complete sentence

5 Cut the sentence from the document

6 Paste the sentence back into the document, in exactly the same place

7 Select three consecutive words

8 Drag-and-drop the three words to another location in the text

9 Insert the omega symbol (Ω) after the second word of the text

10 Insert the telephone symbol (☎) from Wingdings font after this

3   Formatting text

About formatting

When you first enter text at the keyboard in Word it is generally unformatted. That is, it is plain, unembellished, with no changes applied to alter its appearance. Generally, it will be in the default font (say, Times New Roman) and a default size (say, 12 point).

Making alterations to text's appearance is known as *formatting* the text. There are several ways this can be done in Word:

❐ formatting can be applied by the user to individual or grouped characters — this is known as *character formatting*

❐ formatting can be applied by the user to whole paragraphs — called (fancy that) *paragraph formatting*

❐ formatting can be applied automatically by Word — either as you enter text or afterwards, and either across a whole document (using Word's *AutoFormat* feature), or to paragraphs (using *paragraph styles*).

While character and paragraph formatting are both very powerful tools and can give you the visual effects you might require in a document, the *real* power of a word processor like Word lies in its ability to apply automatic formatting.

Take note

Use character and paragraph formatting by all means — and they're going to be described over the next few pages so you can get to grips with them — but bear in mind that only when you use them to build automatic formatting features do they really become useful

You can format whole lines

You can format individual characters or words

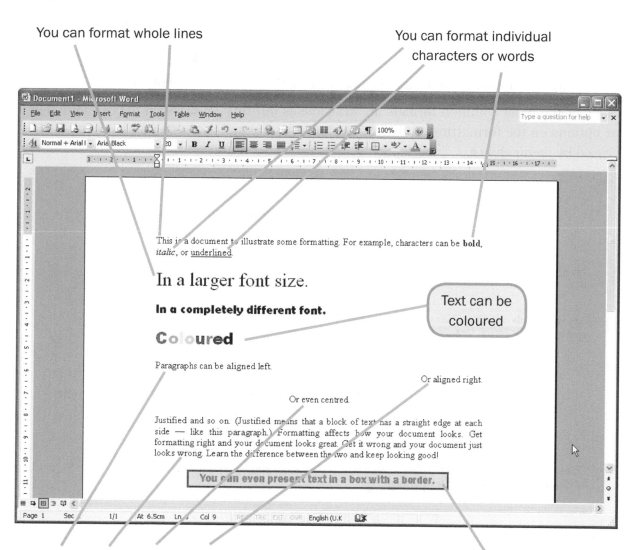

This is a document to illustrate some formatting. For example, characters can be **bold**, *italic*, or underlined.

In a larger font size.

In a completely different font.

Coloured

Text can be coloured

Paragraphs can be aligned left.

Or aligned right.

Or even centred.

Justified and so on. (Justified means that a block of text has a straight edge at each side — like this paragraph.) Formatting affects how your document looks. Get formatting right and your document looks great. Get it wrong and your document just looks wrong. Learn the difference between the two and keep looking good!

You can even present text in a box with a border.

Paragraphs can be aligned to suit

Borders and shades can be applied to paragraphs

Tip

Formatting is the key to producing good-looking, effective documents. Learn how to do the job properly and your documents will always be admired. There's no art to formatting — just about everything you need to know is included here in this book. Learn all the techniques of formatting covered here and never look back

Character formats

Character formatting is a matter of selecting the text you wish to format, then applying the format change you want.

Many of the most common formats are available as buttons or options on the formatting toolbar. Some, however, are accessed by menu choice.

> **1** Select the text to be formatted — this can be an individual letter, a word, group of words, sentence, paragraph, or even the whole document

This is a sample of text in Times New Roman font at 10 point. It will be used to **illustrate chara**[ter formatting].

> **2** Format the selected text to suit — this example shows the selected text emboldened

This is a sample of text in Times New Roman font at 10 point. It will be used to **illustrate character formatting**

Text is displayed formatted on screen. What-you-see on-screen is more-or-less what-you-get on printout

Tip

To format a single word you don't need to select the word in the usual manner — all you have to do is click anywhere in the word, then apply the format changes you want

Basic steps

There are three main ways you can apply formatting to text:

1 From the formatting tool-bar — buttons or options

cont...

Click buttons to apply (or remove) bold, italic, and underline

1 The formatting toolbar gives the easiest options to change common formats

Normal ▾ Times New Roman ▾ 12 ▾ **B** *I* U

Change font size with this drop-down list box

Change font with this drop-down list box — if you have many fonts in your system you can jump in the list by entering the font's initial letter in the font name box — the list jumps di-rectly to fonts with that initial letter for you to select

If the font size you want isn't listed, just enter your desired size at the keyboard — most fonts will display and print correctly for just about any size you want

12 ▾

8
9
10
11
12
14
16
18
20
22
24
26

Franklin Gothic Demi ▾

T Franklin Gothic Demi
T Stone Sans OS ITC TT-Bold
T Arial Black
T Berlin Sans FB Demi
T Agency FB
T ALGERIAN
T Arial
T Arial Black
T Arial Narrow
T Arial Rounded MT Bold
T Arial Unicode MS
T *Arioso BT*

The fonts you've used most recently are listed in the top of the list, above this line

All fonts are listed alphabetically below the line

Character formats (cont)

2 From the **Font** dialog box (choose **Format→Font**, or type `Alt`+`O` then `F` to display it)

The **Font** dialog box gives some more formatting options

Click this tab to see more options regarding letter spacing and vertical positioning

List box for font size

List box for available fonts

Drop-down list box holding available colours to format text with

List box of bold and italic format options

Check box options for various formats

Preview box, to see the effects of formats you have selected

Drop-down list box for special underlining effects

Font dialog box contents:

Tabs: Font | Character Spacing | Text Effects

Font: Franklin Gothic Demi
- Franklin Gothic Demi
- Franklin Gothic Demi Cond
- Franklin Gothic Heavy
- Franklin Gothic Medium
- Franklin Gothic Medium Cond

Font style: Regular
- Regular
- Italic
- Bold
- Bold Italic

Size: 12
- 8
- 9
- 10
- 11
- 12

Font color: Automatic
Underline style: (none)
Underline color: Automatic

Effects
- ☐ Strikethrough
- ☐ Double strikethrough
- ☐ Superscript
- ☐ Subscript
- ☐ Shadow
- ☐ Outline
- ☐ Emboss
- ☐ Engrave
- ☐ Small caps
- ☐ All caps
- ☐ Hidden

Preview

Franklin Gothic Demi

This is a TrueType font. This font will be used on both printer and screen.

Default... | OK | Cancel

3 With keyboard combinations. These can very often provide the quickest methods of applying formats

Keyboard shortcut combinations

Many formatting options can best be applied with a keyboard shortcut:

Bold	`Ctrl`+`B`
Italic	`Ctrl`+`I`
Underline	`Ctrl`+`U`
Word underline....................................	`Ctrl`+`Shift`+`W`
Double underline	`Ctrl`+`Shift`+`D`
Subscript	`Ctrl`+`=`
Superscript	`Ctrl`+`Shift`+`=`
Small caps	`Ctrl`+`Shift`+`K`
All caps	`Ctrl`+`Shift`+`A`
Change case	`Shift`+`S`
Hidden text	`Ctrl`+`Shift`+`H`
Copy formats	`Ctrl`+`Shift`+`C`
Paste formats	`Ctrl`+`Shift`+`V`
Remove formats..................................	`Ctrl`+spacebar
Font	`Ctrl`+`Shift`+`F`
Symbol font	`Ctrl`+`Shift`+`Q`
Point size	`Ctrl`+`Shift`+`P`
next up	`Ctrl`+`>`
next down................................	`Ctrl`+`<`
up one point	`Ctrl`+`]`
down one point	`Ctrl`+`[`

Tip

You can apply a format to the insertion point too. This way, anything you type after the format is applied has that format, until you change it again. This is useful for, say, italicising a single word for emphasis as you type it — just apply the italic format (say, type `Ctrl`+`I`) before you type the word, then remove the italic format (type `Ctrl`+`I` again) hence returning to regular text after the word is finished

Painting a format

If you see text which is formatted the way you want another selection of text to be formatted, you can copy the formatting onto further text with the Format Painter button on the Standard toolbar.

1 Select the text, part of text, or simply position the insertion point anywhere inside the text you wish to copy the formatting from

2 Click the format painter button ✍ on the Standard toolbar. The pointer changes to the format painter pointer 🖌I

3 Select the text you want to be formatted with that format

> **1** Select the text with the format you want to copy (in this case an italicised word)

Take it from me. There's no *point* in trying to pass your driving test. Within ten years at most — more likely five — there'll be so many cars on the road that no-one will be able to drive more than 35 miles per hour anyway. And where's the fun in that?

Tip

Removing a character format follows the same procedure as applying it in the first place. You first select the text, then you go through the same steps you took to originally apply it. If a word is emboldened, for example, you simply select it then click the bold button **B** on the formatting toolbar to remove the format

2 Click

3 Select the text to be formatted

Take it from me. There's no *point* in trying to pass your driving test. Within ten years at most — more likely five — there'll be so many cars on the road that no-one will be able to drive more than 35 miles an hour anyway. And where's the fun in that?

Once selected, the text is automatically formatted

Take it from me. There's no *point* in trying to pass your driving test. Within ten years at most — more likely five — there'll be so many cars on the road that no-one will be able to *drive more than 35 miles per hour* anyway. And where's the fun in that?

Tip

You don't even need to select a single word if you want to paint another word's format onto it with the format painter pointer. Just click anywhere inside the word and the format is painted over the whole word

Tip

If you *double-click* the format painter button after selecting text with the format you want to copy, the format painter pointer remains active after you have painted the format to further text. You can continue to paint the format for as long as you want onto more selections of text. Click the format painter button again to de-activate the format painter pointer

Paragraph formats

Whereas character formats affect just the *characters* you select, paragraph formats control the — you've got it — *paragraphs*. In other words, complete blocks of text and their line spacings, indents or alignments for example, are affected by paragraph formats. Paragraph formats *do not just affect* single characters, words, or sentences.

Paragraph marks (¶) indicate where a paragraph ends

This·is·a·left-aligned·paragraph.¶

This·is·a·right-aligned·paragraph.¶

This·is·a·centred·paragraph.¶

This·paragraph·has·single·line-spacing·and·is·indented·by·a· small·amount·on·its·first·line.·Lines·are·close·together,·set·by· Word·itself.·This·is·a·standard·setting·unless·you·change·the· default·style·(covered·later·in·the·book).¶

This·paragraph·has·double·line-spacing·and·is·indented·

on·its·first·line·by·a·slightly·larger·amount.·Lines·are·obviously·

wider·apart·than·the·previous·paragraph.·It's·possible·to·do·this·

all·in·Word·quite·simply·when·you·know·what·you·are·doing.¶

Note that while all these paragraphs in this screenshot of a Word document have the same character formats (they are all in the same font, size, and so on) they still appear different, because their paragraph formats are different

Paragraph marks (¶) are used by Word to store a paragraph's formatting

Take note

A paragraph is defined as any block of text — no matter how short, or how long — ending with a paragraph mark ¶. A paragraph mark is added to your text each time you press Enter or ↵ .

Paragraph marks may be hidden — to display them (or hide them if they are currently displayed) click the Show/Hide ¶ button ¶ on the Standard toolbar

Basic steps

1 First select the paragraph or paragraphs you intend to format

2 Apply the new paragraph format or formats

To apply a paragraph format to a paragraph you use the same techniques you use to apply a character format to a character.

1 Select the paragraph or paragraphs (in this example there are two paragraphs) you want to format

Here·we·go,·here·we·go,·here·we·go.·It's·another·fine,·fine·day·down·at·the·ranch.·The·brunch·is·cooking·and·the·horses·are·lively.·After·we've·eaten·we'll·get·going·and·round·up·the·cattle.·Never·in·the·field·of·human·conflict·has·so·much·been·eaten·by·so·few.¶

Inevitably,·there·will·be·a·cut·in·resources.·There's·now·so·little·money·to·go·round·that's·it's·just·a·question·of·jobs·or·the·tools·to·do·these·jobs.·If·we·want·to·maintain·current·levels·of·employment,·we'll·all·just·have·to·do·with·less·to·spend.¶

Take note

You don't have to select a whole paragraph before you apply formatting to it. If you position the insertion point anywhere within the paragraph then apply formatting the entire paragraph is formatted

Tip

If you are currently typing text into a formatted paragraph, then press Enter or ⏎, the new paragraph so created continues with the format of the preceding paragraph. In other words, if you have formatted a paragraph to the style you want, each subsequent paragraph has the same format

2 Apply the paragraph formats — here the paragraphs have been indented on their first lines and justified

Here· we· go,· here· we· go,· here· we· go.· It's· another· fine,· fine· day· down· at· the· ranch.· The· brunch· is· cooking· and· the· horses· are· lively.· After· we've· eaten· we'll· get· going· and· round· up· the· cattle.· Never· in· the· field· of· human· conflict· has· so· much· been· eaten·by·so·few.¶

Inevitably,· there· will· be· a· cut· in· resources.· There's· now· so· little· money· to· go· round· that's· it's· just· a· question· of· jobs· or· the· tools· to· do· these· jobs.· If· we· want· to· maintain· current· levels· of· employment,·we'll·all·just·have·to·do·with·less·to·spend.¶

Paragraph formats (cont)

Like character formats, paragraph formats can be applied to text in three main ways.

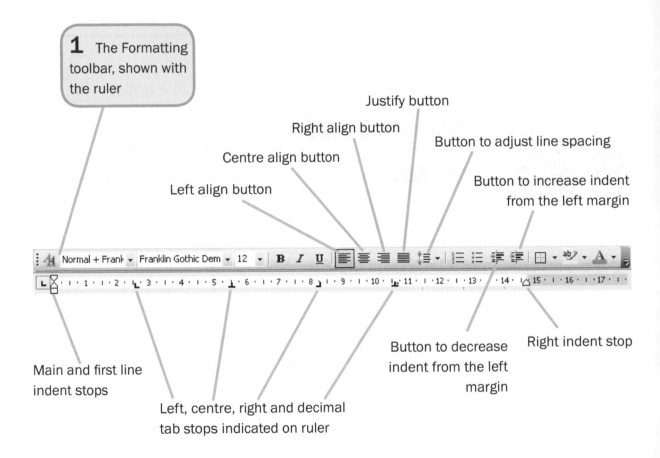

1 The Formatting toolbar, shown with the ruler

Justify button

Right align button

Button to adjust line spacing

Centre align button

Button to increase indent from the left margin

Left align button

Main and first line indent stops

Button to decrease indent from the left margin

Right indent stop

Left, centre, right and decimal tab stops indicated on ruler

2 Formats can be applied from the **Paragraph** dialog box (to display it choose **Format⤷ Paragraph**, or type [Alt]+[O] then [P])

cont...

2 The **Paragraph** dialog box, from which many paragraph formatting options can be set as one step

Click this tab for special text flow options (see over)

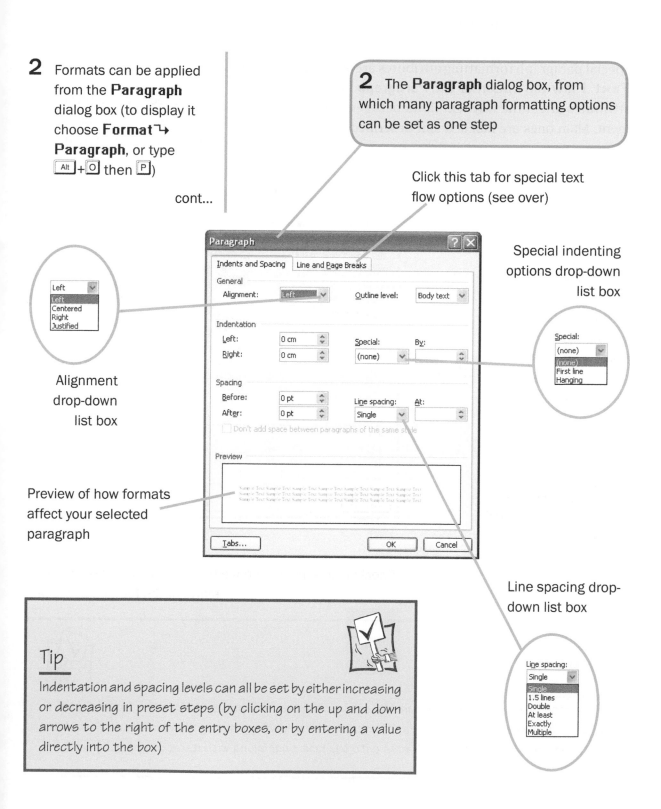

Alignment drop-down list box

Special indenting options drop-down list box

Preview of how formats affect your selected paragraph

Line spacing drop-down list box

Tip

Indentation and spacing levels can all be set by either increasing or decreasing in preset steps (by clicking on the up and down arrows to the right of the entry boxes, or by entering a value directly into the box)

Paragraph formats (cont)

Special paragraph formatting attributes are available from the **Text Flow** tab option of the **Paragraph** dialog box. These attributes affect the way text flows between pages of a document. Main ones are labelled and described.

Checking this prevents a paragraph from being split from the following paragraph

Checking this check box prevents the last line of a paragraph from being printed at the top of a page (a *widow*), or the first line of a paragraph from being printed alone at the bottom of a page (an *orphan*)

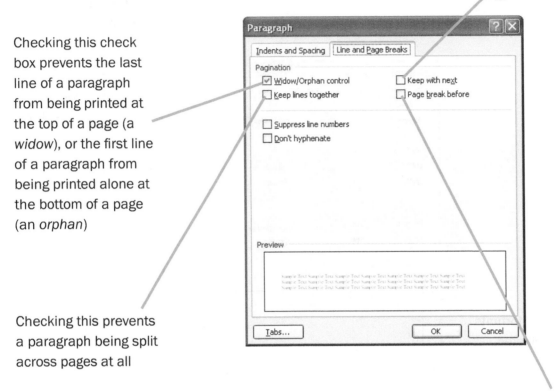

Checking this prevents a paragraph being split across pages at all

Checking this inserts a page break before a paragraph (so it starts at the top of a new page)

Tip

These attributes can make a document look much better and prevent anomalies. If the Keep with Next option is checked for a paragraph formatted as a heading which by chance falls at the bottom of a page, for example, it will be forced onto the next page along with its accompanying text

Basic steps

3 Paragraph formats can be applied directly with keyboard shortcut combinations. Like character formatting keyboard combinations, these are very often the quickest ways of applying certain formats.

Keyboard shortcut combinations

Left-align text	`Ctrl`+`B`
Centre align text	`Ctrl`+`E`
Right-align text	`Ctrl`+`R`
Justify text	`Ctrl`+`J`
Indent from left margin	`Ctrl`+`M`
Decrease indent	`Ctrl`+`Shift`+`M`
Create a hanging indent	`Ctrl`+`T`
Decrease a hanging indent	`Ctrl`+`Shift`+`T`
1 line space	`Ctrl`+`1`
1.5 line space	`Ctrl`+`5`
2 line space	`Ctrl`+`2`
Add or remove 12 points of space before a paragraph	`Ctrl`+`0`
Remove paragraph formats not applied by a style	`Ctrl`+`Q`
Restore Normal style	`Ctrl`+`Shift`+`N`
Display or hide non-printing characters (¶ and so on)	`Ctrl`+`*`

Tip

You can most quickly indent selected paragraphs using either the keyboard shortcut combinations above right, or (even better) using the Decrease Indent or Increase Indent buttons on the Formatting toolbar.

While changes due to either of these methods are in fixed increments you can always later change them by dragging indent markers on the ruler

Take note

While character and paragraph formats are all very nice, and very good, and used properly can greatly improve the look of a document, bear in mind you have to apply every one of them individually.

On the other hand, you can apply formats automatically by using styles (page 102). Automatic formatting is much quicker and, because you can use both methods across documents, ensures that documents you create can have a unified style, or set of styles, giving a much more professional appearance to your work

Tabs

Just like a typewriter, any word processor has the ability to define tab stops. These are used to help align text, such that tables or columns of figures, say, can be neatened up and aligned underneath each other.

Better than a typewriter, on the other hand, word processors usually have more than just one type of tab stop. Where typewriters only align text so that text is left-aligned after the tab stop, Word allows text to be:

❏ left-aligned — as on a typewriter, with text aligned after the tab stop

❏ centre-aligned — with text centred around the tab stop

❏ right-aligned — where text is aligned-right to the tab stop

❏ decimal-aligned — with monetary figures, say, aligned so their decimal point is aligned directly on the tab stop

❏ bar-aligned — Word creates a vertical line in your document, the height of the text line, at the tab stop.

In addition, you can control where lines of text indent this way too.

The most straightforward way of setting tabs is with the ruler.

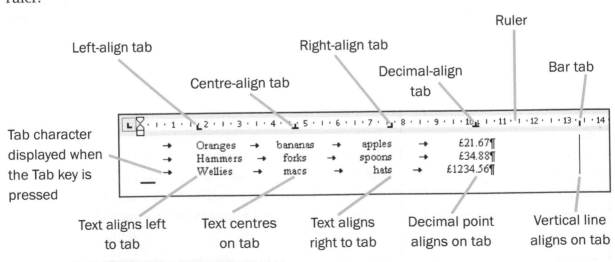

Ruler

Left-align tab

Centre-align tab

Right-align tab

Decimal-align tab

Bar tab

Tab character displayed when the Tab key is pressed

→	Oranges	→	bananas	→	apples	→	£21.67¶
→	Hammers	→	forks	→	spoons	→	£34.88¶
→	Wellies	→	macs	→	hats	→	£1234.56¶

Text aligns left to tab

Text centres on tab

Text aligns right to tab

Decimal point aligns on tab

Vertical line aligns on tab

Basic steps

1 Repeatedly click the Tab Alignment button (the default is [∟]) until the type of tab you require is displayed

[∟] — align left

[⊥] — align centre

[⌐] — align right

[⊥] — align to decimal point

[|] — align to bar

[▽] — first line indent

[⊔] — hung indent

2 Click in the ruler at the position you want the tab stop. It is displayed in the ruler as a symbol (according to which tab stop type you selected

3 Adjust the tab stop if you need, by dragging it along the ruler to its new position

Take note

Tabs are a paragraph format. In other words, they are set for and remain in force for a paragraph — no matter how many lines the paragraph runs to

Take note

Even if you don't put in your own tab stops, there are default tab stops in any Word document — just press [↵] and see

1 The Tab Alignment button — keep clicking it until the tab stop you want is selected (align left is default)

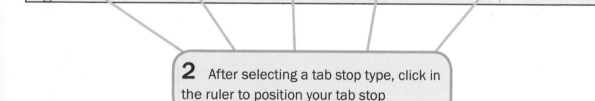

2 After selecting a tab stop type, click in the ruler to position your tab stop

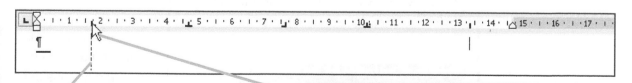

As you drag, a line shows you the new tab position in the document

3 You can adjust a tab stop's position by dragging it along the ruler to where you want it

Borders and shading

Two other paragraph formats which can be used to create a professional appearance to Word documents are paragraph borders and shading.

Borders are rules around a paragraph (which may, or may not, be thick enough to see — a border of zero thickness is still there, albeit not visible). Shadings are the background shades of colours or greys which go inside borders.

Borders are set up and adjusted in one of three ways:

❏ with the Borders button on the Formatting toolbar

❏ through the Tables & Borders toolbar

❏ with the Paragraph Borders and Shading dialog box.

The simplest way — shown here — is with the Tables & Borders toolbar.

1 If it's not already displayed, call up the Tables & Borders toolbar by clicking the Borders button on the Standard toolbar (or right-click any toolbar and check the **Tables & Borders** checkbox)

How the paragraph is formatted is very important to how the bordered and shaded paragraph will look. Justified or centred text always looks better than left- or right-aligned text, simply because the borders (and resultant shading) are evenly placed around the text

Borders can be:
- ■ thinner
- ■ thicker
- ■ non-existent

Here is a bordered paragraph — I think it looks really smart. If text is justified — which this is, or centred, it gives a tidy appearance at each side.

Here is another paragraph — this time though aligned left to see the difference. Not so good, hmm? I agree. However, what do you think of the shading?

Here is a paragraph with no border but some shading. As the shading is quite dark, the text colour has been reversed to white creating a nice effect.

For a paragraph you intend to shade darkly, consider reversing text to create a pleasant effect

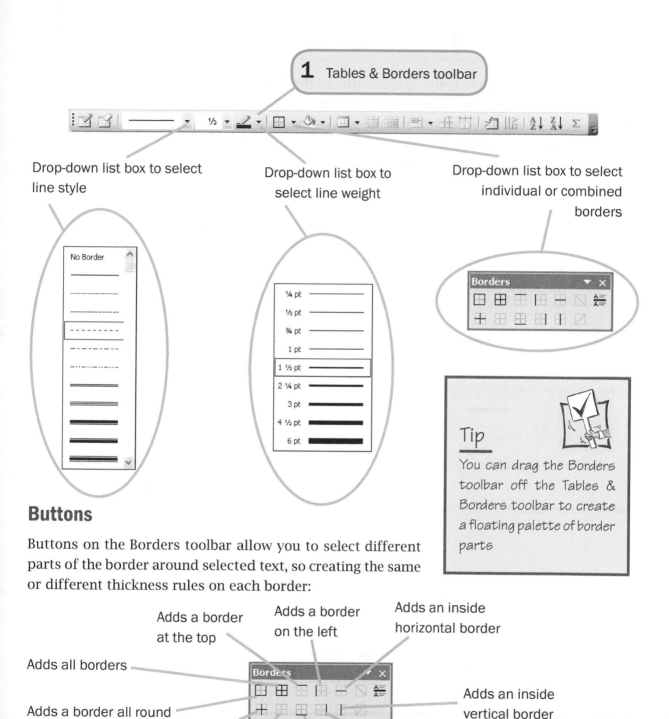

1 Tables & Borders toolbar

Drop-down list box to select line style

Drop-down list box to select line weight

Drop-down list box to select individual or combined borders

No Border

¼ pt
½ pt
¾ pt
1 pt
1 ½ pt
2 ¼ pt
3 pt
4 ½ pt
6 pt

Borders

Tip

You can drag the Borders toolbar off the Tables & Borders toolbar to create a floating palette of border parts

Buttons

Buttons on the Borders toolbar allow you to select different parts of the border around selected text, so creating the same or different thickness rules on each border:

Adds a border at the top

Adds a border on the left

Adds an inside horizontal border

Adds all borders

Adds a border all round

Adds inside borders

Borders

Adds an inside vertical border

Removes all borders

Adds a border at the bottom

Adds a border on the right

Borders & shading (cont)

When you add a border to text it extends around the *full size* of the paragraph. In other words, whatever the width and height of the paragraph, the border is the same — regardless of whether the text itself totally fills the border. This can result in unusual (and unattractive) borders.

Basic steps

1 Click in the paragraph to be bordered

2 Select the style and weight of border, and shading colour required

3 Apply the border

4 Adjust the right indent of the paragraph to the text width

1 Select the text to have a border — remember (as borders and shades are paragraph formats) you only need to click in the paragraph to select the whole paragraph

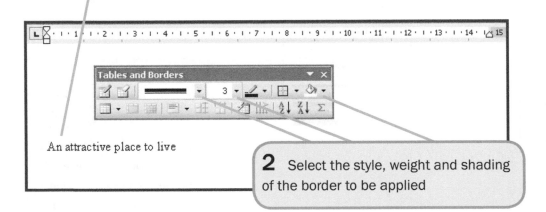

An attractive place to live

2 Select the style, weight and shading of the border to be applied

3 Apply the border — this one is a boxed border, applied with the boxed border button

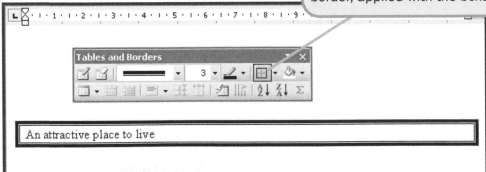

An attractive place to live

4 Drag the right indent marker of the ruler in, until the indent is just to the right of the text in the paragraph

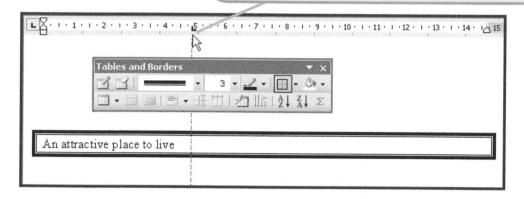

An attractive place to live

The paragraph is now boxed properly and attractively — note that if you now add to the text in the bordered paragraph the border will still be the correct width as the text simply overflows onto the next line which is of the same width. The border's bottom rule remains below the bottom line of the paragraph however many lines it has

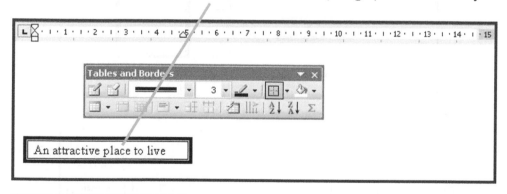

An attractive place to live

Tip

The procedure for applying a border is to first select the text to be bordered, next select the thickness of border, then finally apply the border

Tip

Remember that borders and shadings are paragraph formats. All paragraph formats can be selected automatically with a style — see page 102. As a result, you can create bordered and shaded paragraphs to your exact specifications very quickly if you preset them as styles

Borders & shading (cont)

You can create and adjust borders and shadings through the Borders and Shading dialog box too. While this isn't as quick as using the Borders toolbar it does provide some options not otherwise available.

Basic steps

1 To call up the **Borders and Shading** dialog box choose **Format⤷ Borders and Shading**, or type [Alt]+[O] then [B]

1 The **Borders and Shading** dialog box

Click this tab to see the shading options (see opposite)

Preview

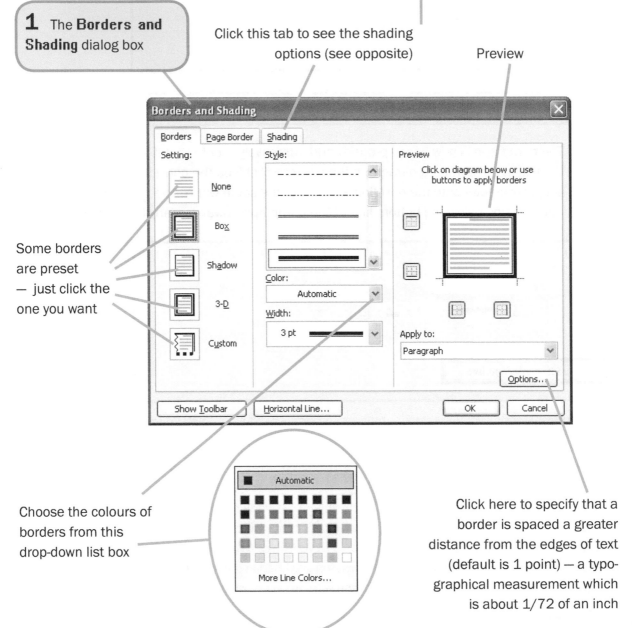

Some borders are preset — just click the one you want

Choose the colours of borders from this drop-down list box

Click here to specify that a border is spaced a greater distance from the edges of text (default is 1 point) — a typographical measurement which is about 1/72 of an inch

Click this tab to get back to
borders options

You can display the
Borders toolbar (if it's
not already displayed) by
clicking this button

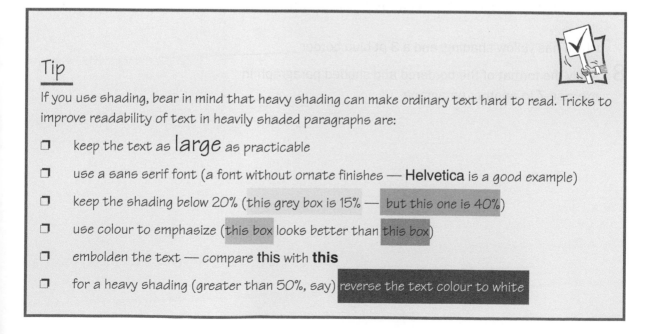

Select fill colour   Select fill style

Tip

If you use shading, bear in mind that heavy shading can make ordinary text hard to read. Tricks to
improve readability of text in heavily shaded paragraphs are:

☐ keep the text as large as practicable

☐ use a sans serif font (a font without ornate finishes — Helvetica is a good example)

☐ keep the shading below 20% (this grey box is 15% — but this one is 40%)

☐ use colour to emphasize (this box looks better than this box)

☐ embolden the text — compare this with **this**

☐ for a heavy shading (greater than 50%, say) reverse the text colour to white

Exercises

1 In a new blank document, type several sentences and paragraphs of text, select the first, change its font colour to red, change the font to Arial, change the font size to 24 pt, make it bold and italic

2 Using the format painter tool, apply the format of that sentence to another sentence

3 Display paragraph marks (hint: by clicking the show/hide ¶ button)

4 Select a paragraph, then indent it by 1 cm from the left and 2 cm from the right, and put a space after it of 8 pt

5 Create a table like this:

cups	saucers	spoons	£2.22
knives	forks	beakers	£10.55
alphabet	spaghetti	beans	£444.77

6 Align the last column of the table to the decimal point

7 Create a bordered and shaded paragraph like this:

This is a bordered and shaded paragraph

which has yellow shading, and a 3 pt blue border

8 Apply the format of the bordered and shaded paragraph in exercise 7 to another paragraph

4 Sections and pages

About sections

Sometimes when you are working on a document, you need to split it up into smaller parts, without splitting it up into totally different documents. These smaller parts are called *sections*.

You only need to create sections if you want to change the appearance of parts of your document in certain ways. The changes you can make within a document which require that sections have to be created include:

❐ a different page size

❐ different margins (page 71)

❐ a different header or footer (page 74)

❐ different line numberings (page 78)

❐ a different number of columns (page 80).

In normal view (and in page layout view if the Show/Hide ¶ button ¶ on the Standard toolbar is clicked), a section end is displayed as shown below.

A section break, indicated by a dotted line. This does not print

---

The quiet revolution
The personal computer world is in a state of limbo as Intel's domination of the market is about to be challenged.

···Section Break (Next Page)··

Things move pretty quickly where personal computers are concerned. From the dawn of the personal computer era just twelve years ago several generations of integrated circuits have come and gone, tens of computer manufacturers have made fortunes and bitten the dust, and just a handful of manufacturers now seems to survive. But that's by no means an end to the story. This year there's the start of what will come to be seen as the biggest shake-up ever know in the industry, with conventions overthrown and market percentages re-negotiated to an extent never seen before. Yet users could be forgiven for not even realizing what's going on. Most of the changes have occurred so far in the mainstream background, with little noise and a great deal of stealth.

Basic steps

1 Position the insertion point in your document where you want the new section to be, then choose **Insert⮑Break**, or type `Alt`+`I` then `B`, to call up the **Break** dialog box

2 Click the button corresponding to the section break you want:

- ▪ **Next Page** — the section break causes the document to force following text to appear at the top of the next page

- ▪ **Even Page** — following text is forced to the top of the next even page of the document

- ▪ **Odd page** — following text is forced to the top of the next odd page of the document

- ▪ **Continuous** — following text occurs straight under the section break, wherever it occurs on a page

3 Click **OK**

Effectively, the changes listed are parameters you apply much like character and paragraph formats, except they affect the whole section (not just a few characters or paragraphs). Every time you want to change one or more of these parameters in just *part* of your document, you need a new section.

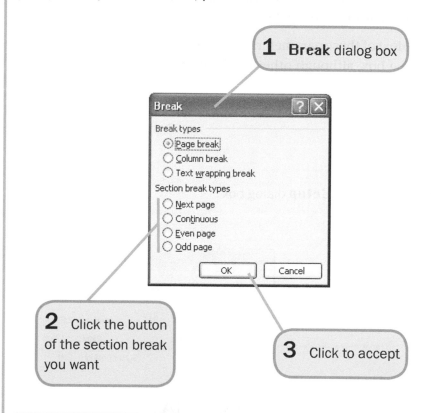

1 **Break** dialog box

2 Click the button of the section break you want

3 Click to accept

Tip

If you don't want parts of your document to be different in any one or more of the ways listed opposite — don't bother using sections.

Put another way — if you want any of the changes listed in just part of your document, you have to use sections

Setting up a document

Apart from character and paragraph formats, a document has other parameters you can format. Where these are contained within a section (or selected sections) of a document they affect just that section (or sections). Where the document contains no section breaks, or where all sections are selected before formatting, the whole document is affected.

Most of these parameters are adjusted from the Page Setup dialog box, although other methods are sometimes available.

Basic steps

1 Choose **File↵Page Setup**, or type `Alt`+`F` then `U`, to call up the **Page Setup** dialog box

2 Click tabs to see the different controls available to adjust parameters

3 If you make any changes to parameters, click **OK** to accept changes, or **Cancel** to ignore them

1 **Page Setup** dialog box

2 Click tabs to bring controls frontmost in the dialog box

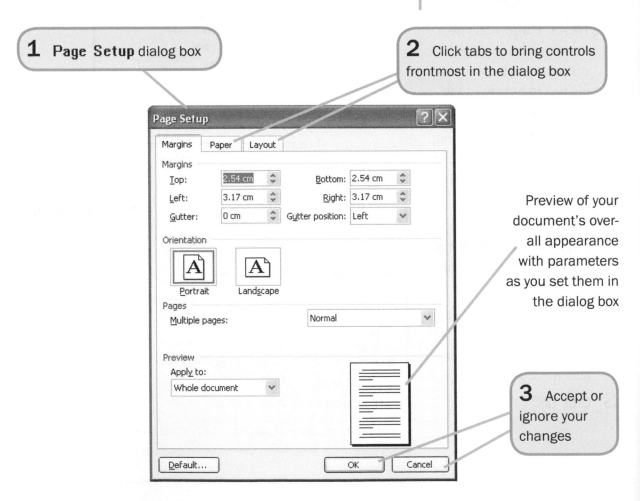

Preview of your document's overall appearance with parameters as you set them in the dialog box

3 Accept or ignore your changes

Margins

Margins are imaginary guides on a document page, outside of which text isn't normally situated. By default, Word creates margins for any new document — usually of 1 inch (2.54 cm) from top and bottom of the page, and 1.25 inches (3.17 cm) from left and right page edge.

You can change margins, either for a whole document or for a section, from the Page Setup dialog box.

Basic steps

1 Choose **File⇨Page Setup**, or type Alt + F then U, to call up the **Page Setup** dialog box

2 Click the **Margins** tab if it's not already frontmost (see opposite)

3 Adjust margin dimensions to suit

Tip

In many of these tabs (and in many other dialog boxes, for that matter) adjustments can be made to some controls by increasing or decreasing in preset steps by clicking on the up or down arrows to the right of the entry boxes. Alternatively, you can click on the entry box you want to change then enter the exact value you want

Take note:

Don't confuse margins with indents:

❏ margins set distances between what you put on a page and the page edges

❏ indents are formats you apply to space the contents around the page

Tip

You can specify that the margin changes be applied to just the section you are in, from the current point on (Word places a section break at the insertion point and changes apply to the section following it), or the whole document, from the drop-down list box on the Margins tab of the Page Setup dialog box

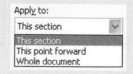

Margins (cont)

Some of the controls of the Margins tab of the Page Setup dialog box allow you to control how pages are printed for double-sided purposes (that is, for the likes of books and reports).

1 If the document is to be double-sided, tick the **Mirror Margins** check box

2 Change the **Inside** and **Outside** margins measurements to suit your requirements

3 If you plan to bind your document with a ring or similar method, enter a value in the **Gutter** entry box — this adds extra space to the inside margins to allow for the binding

> **3** Entering a value here creates an extra space to allow for a binding

> **2** Adjust margin measurements

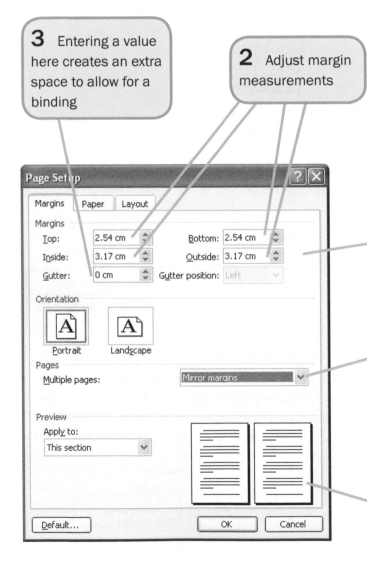

Measurements are shown here in centimetres — you can change units to incheas, millimetres, points or picas (typographical units) in the Options dialog box

> **1** Choose Mirror margins for margins which are equal on the inside and outside of left- and right-hand pages, or top and bottom of above and below pages

Preview always shows the effects of entries and controls

Basic steps

1 Choose `View`→`Page Layout`, or type `Alt`+`V` then `P`, or (best) click the Page Layout button 📄 to view your document in page layout view

2 Drag your margins to suit

Margins in print layout view

As an alternative to using the Page Setup dialog box, you can adjust margins by dragging margin boundaries in page layout view. This is probably faster, though you have little accuracy, you can't specify how much of the document you want to apply changes to (current section, current point forward, or the whole document — dragging from the ruler applies changes to just the current section, or whole document if no section break exists), and mirror margin and gutter margin controls aren't available.

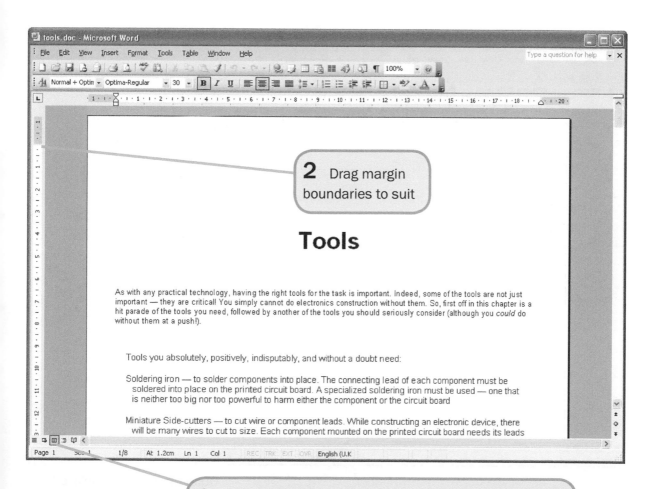

2 Drag margin boundaries to suit

Tools

As with any practical technology, having the right tools for the task is important. Indeed, some of the tools are not just important — they are critical! You simply cannot do electronics construction without them. So, first off in this chapter is a hit parade of the tools you need, followed by another of the tools you should seriously consider (although you *could* do without them at a push!).

Tools you absolutely, positively, indisputably, and without a doubt need:

Soldering iron — to solder components into place. The connecting lead of each component must be soldered into place on the printed circuit board. A specialized soldering iron must be used — one that is neither too big nor too powerful to harm either the component or the circuit board

Miniature Side-cutters — to cut wire or component leads. While constructing an electronic device, there will be many wires to cut to size. Each component mounted on the printed circuit board needs its leads

1 Click here if document is not already in page layout view

Headers and footers

A header is a heading (often called a running head) which appears at the top of each page in a document or section of a document. A footer is at the bottom of each page. You can put text or graphical items in either and you can format them in the usual ways.

Basic steps

1 To create either a header or a footer choose **View→Header and Footer**, or type [Alt]+[V] then [H]. The document changes to page layout view and displays the header entry box and the Header and Footer toolbar

1 Change to Headers and Footers mode

Header entry box — type in what you want and format it to suit

Header and footer toolbar

Jump between the header and footer by clicking here

Click to get back to normal view

Document text is displayed but greyed out

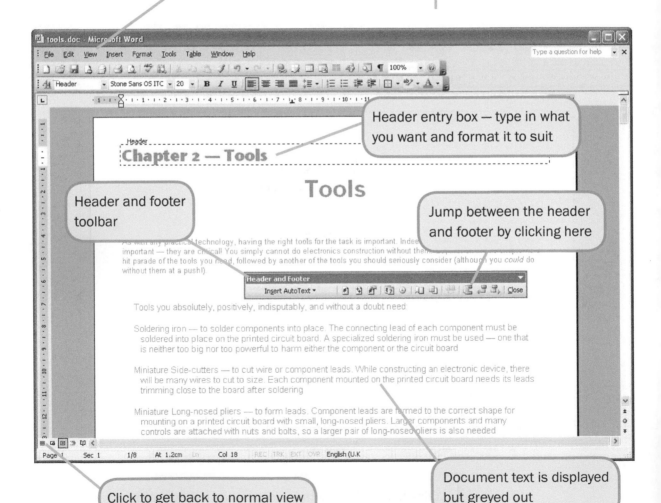

Double-click a background header to make it active

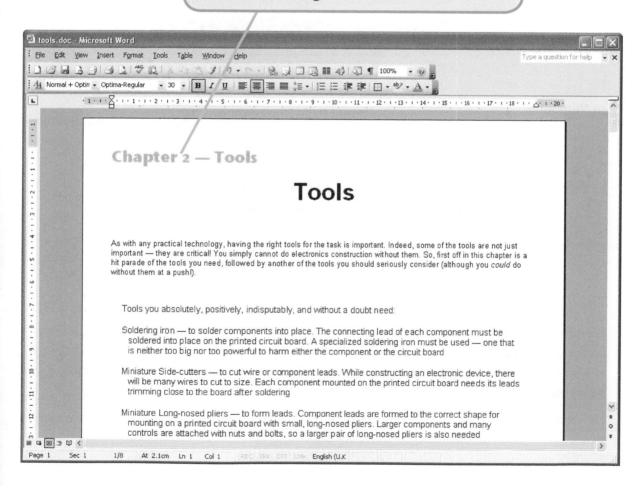

Headers & footers (cont)

The Headers and Footers toolbar has a number of buttons.
Use these to access various features and entries you can make
into a header or footer.

Switch Between Header and Footer
button — click to move from a header
to a footer or back (alternatively, you
can scroll down or up the page in the
document window)

Show/Hide Document Text button — jumps between
document text and header or footer text

Page Setup button — calls up the Page
Setup dialog box

Close — click when you no longer
need the Headers and Footers
toolbar

Current Date, and Current Time

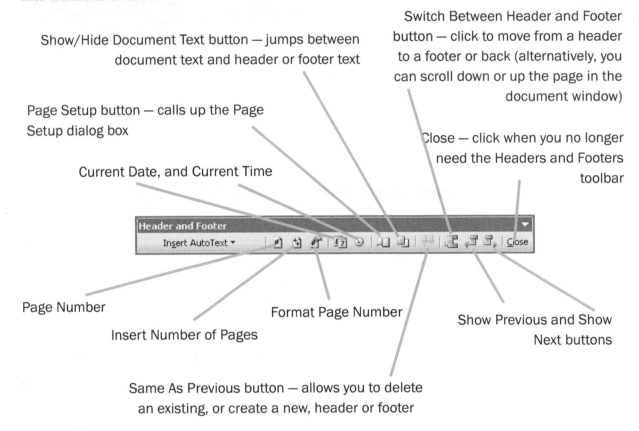

Page Number

Insert Number of Pages

Format Page Number

Show Previous and Show
Next buttons

Same As Previous button — allows you to delete
an existing, or create a new, header or footer

Tip

Remember you can format a header or a footer in exactly the same way you format ordinary text in your document. You can embolden, italicise, underline and so on. You can make it centrally aligned or right aligned if you want. You are not restricted to just one line of text. You can also use a graphical item.

Also remember that each section you create can have its own header and footer — use this feature to set up a header for each chapter of a large document, for example

Basic steps

1 Choose **View**⤷**Page Layout**, or type ⎡Alt⎤+⎡V⎤ then ⎡P⎤, or (best) click the Page Layout button ▤ to view your document in page layout view

2 Double-click the header (or footer) to make it active

3 Drag margin and header (or footer) boundaries to suit

Page layout settings

You can adjust the distance from a page edge taken up by a header at the top of your document page (or the footer at the bottom) from the Page Setup dialog box (the From Edge entries). You can also change margins from here (allowing you to adjust the distance between the header or footer and the document text).

An easier way, however, is to switch to page layout view and drag the various boundaries to suit what you want.

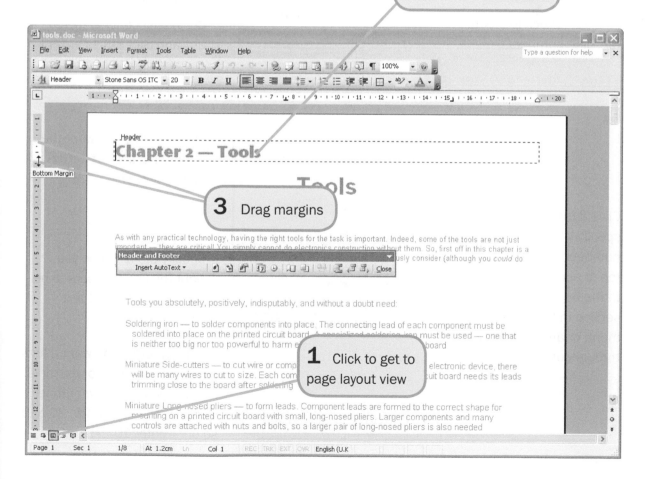

2 Double-click the header to make it active

3 Drag margins

1 Click to get to page layout view

Line numbers

Word can display and print line numbers alongside text. This can be useful in technical documentation, and even required in legal literature.

Line numbers are:

❐ printed in the left margin

❐ not applied to lines in tables, headers, footers and some other parts of a document

❐ only visible on-screen in page layout view (or print preview).

1 Choose **File↵Page Setup**, or type Alt + F then U to call up the **Page Setup** dialog box. Click the **Layout** tab if it's not already frontmost. Next click the **Line Numbers** button to call up the **Line Numbers** dialog box

2 Check the **Add line numbering** check box to create line numbers

3 Adjust controls to suit and click **OK** to accept and view line numbers

2 Check to create line numbers

1 **Line Numbers** dialog box

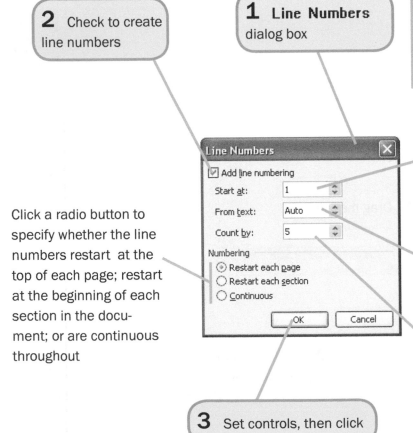

Click a radio button to specify whether the line numbers restart at the top of each page; restart at the beginning of each section in the document; or are continuous throughout

Enter the line you want the numbering to start at (default is line 1)

Specify the distance you want the line numbers to be from the document text

Enter how often you want a line number to occur — for example, if you only want a line number every 10 lines — 10, 20, 30 and so on — enter 10

3 Set controls, then click

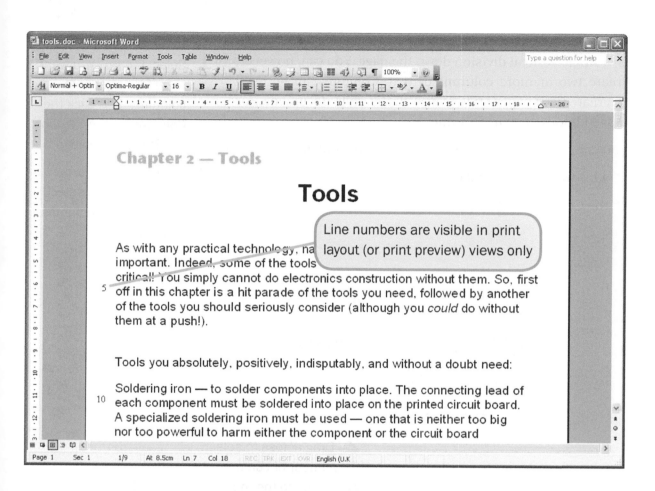

Tip

If you view your work in normal view, and line numbering is enabled, you won't see the numbers until you print.

To remove line numbers from a section or document, you have to uncheck the Add Line Numbering check box in the Line Numbers dialog box.

Just because they are not visible in normal view doesn't mean they are not there!

Take note

To change the format of line numbers you have to redefine a style known as the Line Number style — see Chapter 5 for more information about styles

79

Columns

Generally, text in a Word document is in a single column — that is, a single vertical division down the page. You can, however, create two or more columns of text. Columns can be used to create newspaper-style or newsletter-style documents, or indeed books such as this one.

You can create columns in your document from either:

❑ a button on the Standard toolbar; or

❑ the Columns dialog box.

Basic steps

■ **Standard toolbar**

1 Select the text you want to be formatted into columns, then click the Columns button 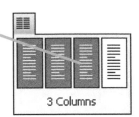 on the Standard toolbar

2 Drag across the drop-down window to select the number of columns you want

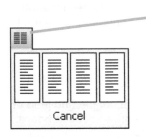

1 Click the Columns button to display this drop-down window

2 Drag across to select the number of columns you want — let go the mouse button to accept

3 Columns

Take note

You can only see columns you create in page layout view or print preview view! In normal view, text is simply displayed at the width of a single column — so if your text is across two columns on the page, normally viewed text will only be a half page wide

Basic steps

■ **Columns dialog box**

1 Select the text you want to be formatted into columns, then choose **Format⇥Columns** to call up the **Columns** dialog box

2 Choose the number of columns you want

3 Change column widths and other controls to suit your requirements (see next page)

Tip

If you select text then format it into columns, Word automatically inserts section breaks before and after the text. This way you can have different numbers of columns in different parts of the document — columns are section parameters, remember

If you simply position the insertion point in your document before formatting into columns (that is, you don't select any text), the whole section (the whole document if no section breaks are present) is formatted

1 **Columns** dialog box

2 Click to select the number of columns from these buttons, or enter the number in the lower box

3 Adjust column widths to suit

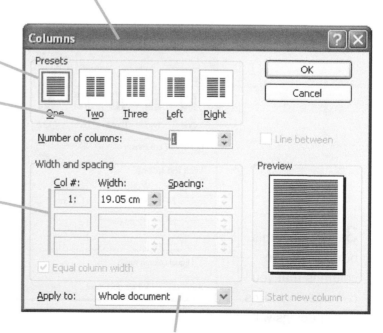

Specify which part of document to apply columns to (whole document, current section, or from this point on)

81

Columns (cont)

If you want to format your section or document into even-width columns, the quickest method is with the Columns button ▦ on the Standard toolbar.

On the other hand, if you want *uneven* columns you have to use the Columns dialog box. This also gives some other controls unavailable with the Columns button:

❐ the spacing between columns

❐ whether a line between columns is displayed

❐ whether the columns apply to the whole document, the current section, or from the current point on.

Basic steps

1 Choose **Format⤷ Columns** to call up the **Columns** dialog box

2 Choose the number of columns you want

3 Uncheck the Equal column width checkbox

4 Adjust column widths and spacing to suit your requirements

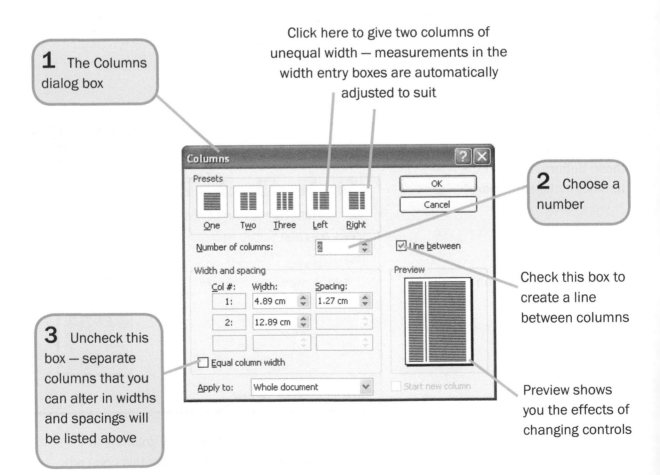

1 The Columns dialog box

Click here to give two columns of unequal width — measurements in the width entry boxes are automatically adjusted to suit

2 Choose a number

Check this box to create a line between columns

3 Uncheck this box — separate columns that you can alter in widths and spacings will be listed above

Preview shows you the effects of changing controls

Tip

You can adjust column widths and the spaces between them by dragging boundaries on the rulers in page layout or print preview views, as shown below. This is often quicker and simpler than from the Columns dialog box, but less accurate.

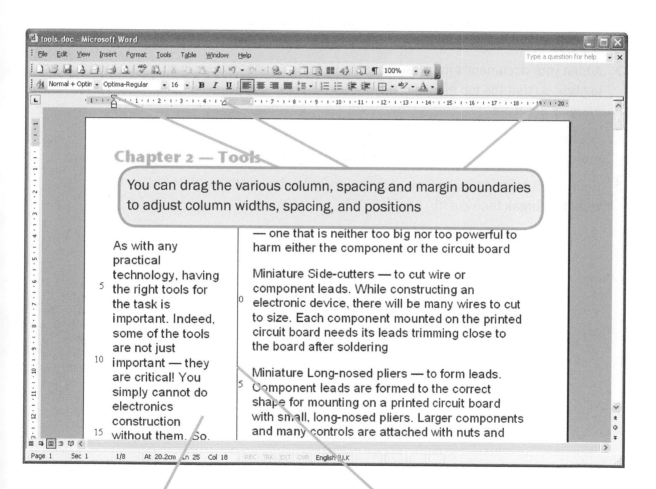

You can drag the various column, spacing and margin boundaries to adjust column widths, spacing, and positions

Chapter 2 — Tools

As with any practical technology, having the right tools for the task is important. Indeed, some of the tools are not just important — they are critical! You simply cannot do electronics construction without them. So,

— one that is neither too big nor too powerful to harm either the component or the circuit board

Miniature Side-cutters — to cut wire or component leads. While constructing an electronic device, there will be many wires to cut to size. Each component mounted on the printed circuit board needs its leads trimming close to the board after soldering

Miniature Long-nosed pliers — to form leads. Component leads are formed to the correct shape for mounting on a printed circuit board with small, long-nosed pliers. Larger components and many controls are attached with nuts and

This document was setup using the controls as entered in the Columns dialog box shown opposite

Line between columns

Exercises

1 In a new blank document, type several sentences and paragraphs of text. Between paragraph 1 and paragraph 2 insert a continuous section break

2 Do the same between paragraph 2 and paragraph 3

3 Make paragraph 2 a three-column paragraph

4 Create a header for your document, and put the current time, and current date into the header

5 Add line numbering to your document, making numbering restart with each new section

6 Adjust your document's margins using the Page Setup dialog box, so that the top margin is 5 cm, while left and right margins are 8 cm

7 Without using the Page Setup dialog box, change the top margin to 2 cm, and the left and right margins to 3 cm

8 Remove all section breaks from your document (hint: select a section break then cut it)

5   Text control

Finding text

Although it probably sounds odd, one of the main jobs a word processor is asked to do in everyday life is to find text. You'd think a word processor had enough coping with all it's asked to do with text without having to actually find the stuff for you too, wouldn't you?

Problem is, in long documents it's not always easy for us to locate specific instances of small pieces of text. Let's say you have worked for weeks and weeks on your latest novel, and you decide that little bit around half way through about your heroine's need for money needs expanding somewhat. What do you do? You could scroll through the book, screen-by-screen, trying to find where it is, but that could take hours — you wrote it weeks ago remember — and you haven't a real idea exactly where it is.

Let Word do the job for you.

Basic steps

1 Choose **Edit↪Find**, or type Alt+E then F, or type Ctrl+F. This calls up the **Find and Replace** dialog box

2 In the **Find what** entry box, type in the text you want to locate

3 If your text contains formats, special characters or other controls, click the **More** button to extend the dialog box

4 Specify the options you want to control the search

5 Click the **Find Next** button to start the search

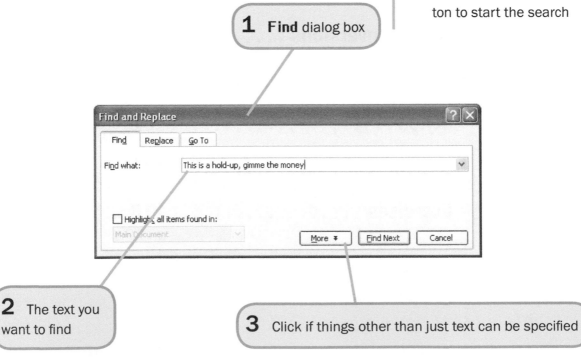

1 **Find** dialog box

2 The text you want to find

3 Click if things other than just text can be specified

Check this to make sure Word looks for the
same capitalization you specify

Find and Replace ? X

Find | Replace | Go To

Find what: | This is a hold-up, gimme the money | ∨

☐ Highlight all items found in:

Main Document ∨ | | Less **±** | | Find Next | | Cancel |

Search Options

Search: | All ∨

☐ Match case
☐ Find whole words only
☐ Use wildcards
☐ Sounds like (English)
☐ Find all word forms (English)

Find

| Format ▾ | | Special ▾ | | No Formatting |

5 Click to start
the search

Specify special parameters for
the search from this drop-
down box

All ∨
Down
Up
All

4 Specify
the options

Specify whether the whole
document is searched, or
which direction the search
takes, with this drop-down box

Font...
Paragraph...
Tabs...
Language...
Frame...
Style...
Highlight

Define the search formats from
this drop-down box — selecting
Font, say, leads you to the **Font**
dialog box

Paragraph Mark
Tab Character
Any Character
Any Digit
Any Letter
Caret Character
§ Section Character
¶ Paragraph Character
Column Break
Em Dash
En Dash
Endnote Mark
Field
Footnote Mark
Graphic
Manual Line Break
Manual Page Break
Nonbreaking Hyphen
Nonbreaking Space
Optional Hyphen
Section Break
White Space

Replacing

In the Find and Replace dialog box you may have noticed a tab marked Replace. Clicking this leads you to the **Replace** dialog box (or you can call up the dialog box directly). This lets you find text in the same way we've seen, then replaces the instances of text with a different text string. Say, your heroine's request for cash doesn't sound too cool, and you want to change it to something with a bit more class. Easy — get Word to replace it.

1 Choose **Edit↳Replace**, or type ⎀Alt⎀+⎀E⎀ then ⎀E⎀, or type ⎀Ctrl⎀+⎀H⎀, or (as we've seen) click the **Replace** tab in the **Find** dialog box. This calls up the **Find and Replace** dialog box

2 Enter the text string to look for

3 Type in the text string to replace it

4 Click the **More** button if you want to specify controls

5 Specify the options (see page 87 for details)

6 Click the **Find Next** button to find the next occurrence of the string, or:

7 Begin the replacements using other buttons

Tip

While Word will happily find and replace text for you (formatted or unformatted) it is equally at home finding and replacing just the formats themselves (ie, without any text associated with them).

So, for example, you can find instances of text which are underlined (<u>a typical typists' method of emphasising text</u>) and replace them all with italicised text (the usual typographers' emphasis method) by specifying the formats to suit. Remember not to enter any text in either of the Find What or Replace With entry boxes

2 The text to be found — leave blank if you're just looking for formats

1 **Find and Replace** dialog box

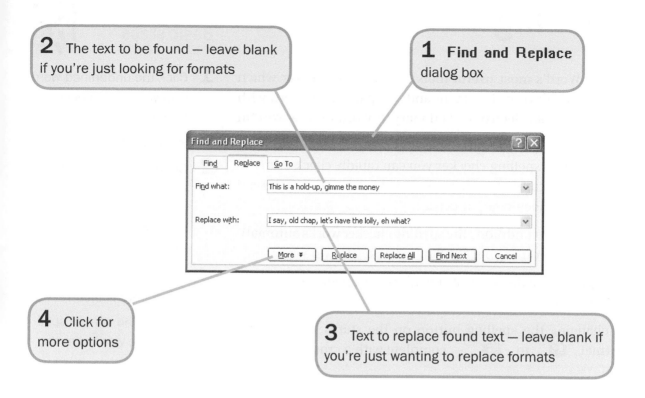

4 Click for more options

3 Text to replace found text — leave blank if you're just wanting to replace formats

6 Click to find the next occurrence of the text

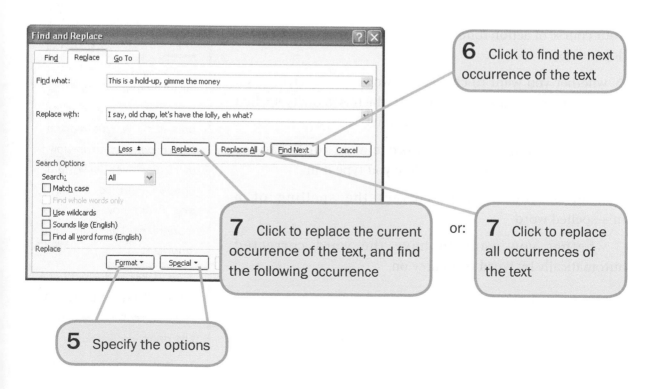

7 Click to replace the current occurrence of the text, and find the following occurrence

or: **7** Click to replace all occurrences of the text

5 Specify the options

Spelling

One of Word's most useful tools is a spelling checker which looks through your document and compares each word with the words in an electronic dictionary. If Word finds a word in the dictionary, it assumes that word is spelled correctly.

Using Word's spelling checker you can rapidly check even the longest of documents — far more quickly than you could read through the document, at least.

Under default conditions the spelling checker works automatically, telling you of your spelling mistakes in two ways:

❏ highlighting the words it considers mis-spelled with a wavy red underline

❏ changing the spelling button on the status bar from its normal 📖 to 📖✗ — complete with a cross.

Making use of Word's spelling checker

Your course of action following notification of a spelling error depends on:

❏ whether you want to change the word at all (maybe it's a person's name, or a scientific word) which is actually spelled correctly but Word hasn't recognized it

❏ whether you want to add the word to Word's dictionary, so it won't be flagged up the next time you type it in

❏ whether you want to correct the spelling of a mis-spelled word

❏ whether you want to have the word corrected automatically by Word from now on.

Basic steps

1 Click the underlined word with your right mouse button

■ **If the word is correct**

2 Choose **Ignore All** from the drop-down menu — the underlined high-lighting is removed from the word (and any other entries of the word)

■ **If the word is incorrect**

3 Choose the correct spelling of the word from the list

Tip

If you type a word regularly which Word incorrectly assumes is mis-spelled, add it to Word's dictionary. From the drop-down menu displayed above right, choose Add to Dictionary. From now on, Word recognizes the word and ignores it.

Also, Word can correct your bad spelling on-the-fly with AutoCorrect — see over the page

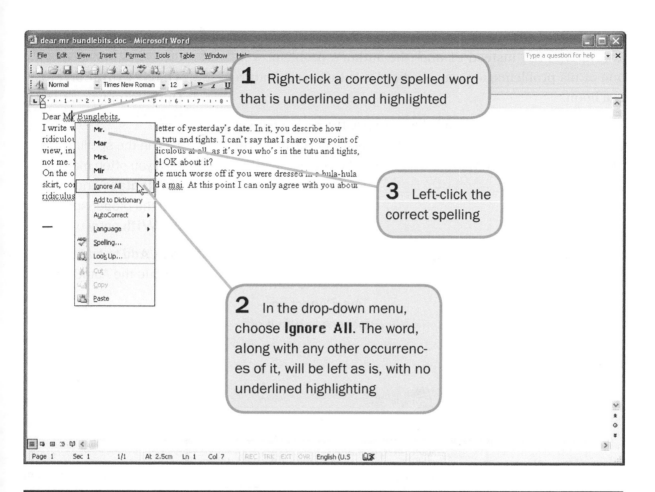

1 Right-click a correctly spelled word that is underlined and highlighted

3 Left-click the correct spelling

2 In the drop-down menu, choose **Ignore All**. The word, along with any other occurrences of it, will be left as is, with no underlined highlighting

Take note

While Word's spelling checker is an extremely useful tool, you must remember that it only compares words in your document with the words in an electronic list dictionary. If words are mis-spelled in-context but in fact make properly spelled words out-of-context, Word still assumes they are spelled correctly. Thus, Word thinks with complements (instead of with compliments) is OK. Remember the anonymous ode:

> I have a spelling checker — it came with my pea see
> It plainly marques four my revue miss steaks eye cannot sea
> I've run this poem threw it, I'm shore your pleased too no
> Its let a perfect inn it's weigh — my checquer told me sew

91

AutoCorrect

If you make the same spelling mistake regularly — say you always type *anf* instead of *and* (the author's problem; well, one of his problems, anyway) — Word's AutoCorrect feature is a boon.

To use AutoCorrect you simply have to specify which mistakes you make, and the correct spelling. Then whenever you make the mistake it is replaced automatically with the correct word.

Basic steps

1 Call up the **AutoCorrect** dialog box by choosing **Tools↦AutoCorrect Options**, or type [Alt]+[T] then [A]

2 Type in the spelling mistake you often make into the **Replace** entry box, and the proper spelling in the **With** entry box

3 Click **Add** to add the word to the AutoCorrect list

4 Click **OK**

1 AutoCorrect dialog box

Check to turn AutoCorrect on — uncheck to turn it off

Other options

2 Mistake you often make, and proper spelling

The AutoCorrect list — scroll through it to view, edit and delete entries

3 Click to add your entries to the AutoCorrect list

4 Click **OK**

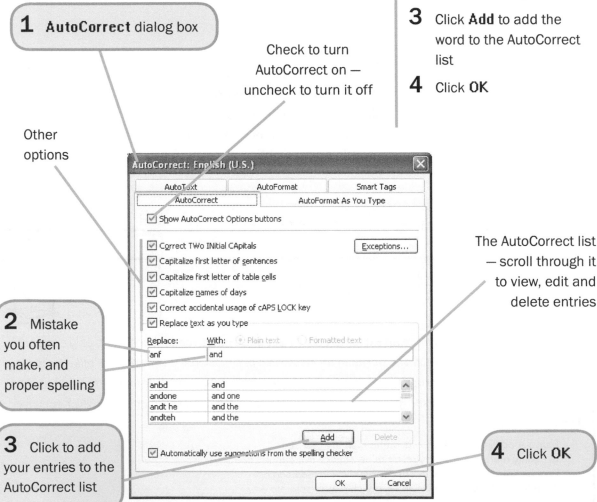

AutoCorrect: English (U.S.)

| AutoText | AutoFormat | Smart Tags |
| AutoCorrect | | AutoFormat As You Type |

☑ Show AutoCorrect Options buttons

☑ Correct TWo INitial CApitals   [Exceptions...]
☑ Capitalize first letter of sentences
☑ Capitalize first letter of table cells
☑ Capitalize names of days
☑ Correct accidental usage of cAPS LOCK key
☑ Replace text as you type

Replace: With: ○ Plain text   ○ Formatted text
| anf | and |

anbd	and
andone	and one
andt he	and the
andteh	and the

[Add] [Delete]

☑ Automatically use suggestions from the spelling checker

[OK] [Cancel]

Remember that you can create an AutoCorrect entry direct from the drop-down menu as you click an underlined highlighted word with your right mouse button.

If you find that Word is finding the same spelling error repeatedly, use the drop-down menu to enter the word automatically into the AutoCorrect list (see page 91)

Tip

AutoCorrect can be used to insert chunks of text into a document when you type a simple keyword. For example, a phrase like 'Yours sincerely', at the end of a letter can have a keyword such as ys. As you type ys and hit the `Enter` or ⏎ key, Word automatically replaces it with the longer phrase.

Phrases up to 255 characters (including spaces and punctuation) are possible, so a considerable amount of boilerplate text (as it's known in the computer business) can be accessed using AutoCorrect. For longer boilerplate text, and items you access less frequently, use Word's AutoText feature instead of AutoCorrect (see over)

Take note

Word detects when you have finished a word — hence knows when to replace it, if it has an AutoCorrect entry — when an end-of-word specifier (usually a space) occurs.

So if the spelling error is followed by another letter, Word doesn't recognise the mistake and cannot correct it with AutoCorrect

Tip

Not only text can be replaced by AutoCorrect entries. Graphics can be included; as can all formatting such as emboldening, sections, borders and shades and so on.

Put your company letterhead into an AutoCorrect entry, and make light work of typing letters

AutoText

Word has the ability to greatly speed-up the entering of text you regularly use in the guise of AutoText.

AutoCorrect, of course (see previous pages), allows you to do this as an automatic — on-the-fly as-you-type — feature. If you don't want it to occur automatically but instead want manual control over automatic insertion of entries, use AutoText.

To use an AutoText entry in your documents, you first have to create it.

Basic steps

- **Creating an entry**

1 Type the text, select it, then choose **Insert⤷ AutoText⤷New**, or type **Alt**+**F3**. This calls up the **Create Auto-Text** dialog box

2 Enter a new name for the entry (if the default name isn't suitable)

3 Click **OK** to accept the new entry

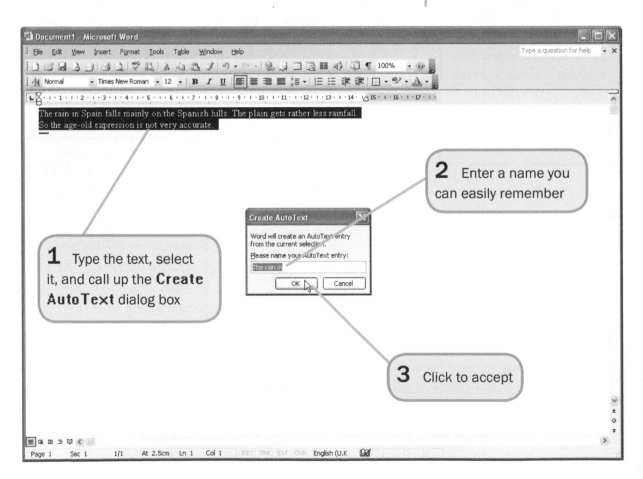

2 Enter a name you can easily remember

1 Type the text, select it, and call up the **Create AutoText** dialog box

3 Click to accept

94

Using an entry

1 When you want to insert an AutoText entry into your document, start to type in the entry name you previously allocated — as you do a screentip is displayed which shows the first few words of the AutoText entry associated with the name

2 Hit ⏎. The entry is inserted into the document

Once your entry is created, you can use it wherever and whenever you want in your documents.

> **1** When you want to insert an AutoText entry, start to type in the entry name...

Sponge
Talking of a soldering iron stand with a sponge, a sponge is actually a very handy accessory to have. Even if you have to resort to — as I have done on occasion — using a simple kitchen sponge, dampen The rain in Spain falls mainly... tea-plate, then so be it!
(Press ENTER to Insert)
The

ScreenTip shows you the AutoText entry associated with the name

> **2** ...then press ⏎

Sponge
Talking of a soldering iron stand with a sponge, a sponge is actually a very handy accessory to have. Even if you have to resort to — as I have done on occasion — using a simple kitchen sponge, dampened with water, stood on a tea-plate, then so be it!

The rain in Spain falls mainly on the Spanish hills. The plain gets rather less rainfall. So the age-old expression is not very accurate.

Tip

As with AutoCorrect, the entries you create for AutoText can include graphical items and text formatting. Like AutoCorrect entries, too, you can use AutoText to insert boilerplate text into your documents.

In fact, the only real difference between AutoText and AutoCorrect as far as the ordinary user — you — is concerned, is how the entries are inserted into your documents.

❑ AutoCorrect entries are inserted automatically, as soon as the entry name is typed.

❑ AutoText entries are inserted semi-automatically — you have to specify that the entry name be replaced with the entry.

They each have their uses

Tables

Earlier in the book we saw how to produce a simple table using tab stops. This is fine for just that — simple tables — but for anything more complex than just a couple of rows and columns things can be made much easier with Word's in-built table feature.

Tables are made up by a collection of *cells*, in rows and columns. Word displays a table in *gridlines* (dotted lines around all the cells of a table) which are not printed and are merely provided on-screen for guidance.

You can add text or graphical elements to cells of a Word table, and you can format text in any character or paragraph format as usual.

You create a table in one of two ways:

❐ from the **Insert Table** dialog box

❐ with the Table button on the Standard toolbar.

Basic steps

■ **Insert Table dialog box**

1 Position the insertion point where you want to create a table, then choose **Table → Insert → Table**, or type [Alt]+[A] then [I]. This calls up the **Insert Table** dialog box

2 Enter the numbers of columns and rows you want

3 Click **OK** to create the table — Word displays the empty table as dotted gridlines

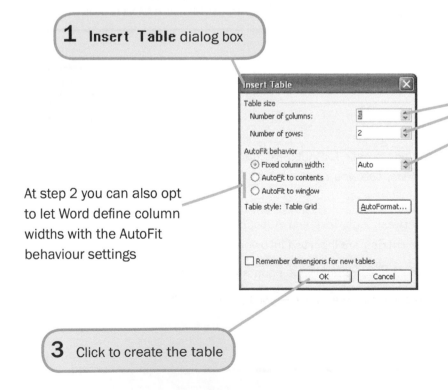

1 Insert Table dialog box

2 Enter number of rows and columns (and column width if you know what you want)

At step 2 you can also opt to let Word define column widths with the AutoFit behaviour settings

3 Click to create the table

 **Insert Table button**

1 Position the insertion point where you want to create a table, then click the Insert Table button  on the Standard toolbar

2 Drag across the drop-down grid to select the number of columns and rows you want, then let go the mouse button

> **1** Click to drop-down the table grid

3 x 4 Table

> **2** Drag across grid to select the number of rows and columns you want

The insertion point is positioned at the top-left cell in the table ready for you to enter text. You move around in a table by clicking the mouse in another cell, tabbing with the `Tab` key, or pressing the `↑``↓``←``→` keys in the direction you want to move.

Press `Tab` to jump to next cell

Press `Shift`+`Tab` to jump to previous cell

Gridlines

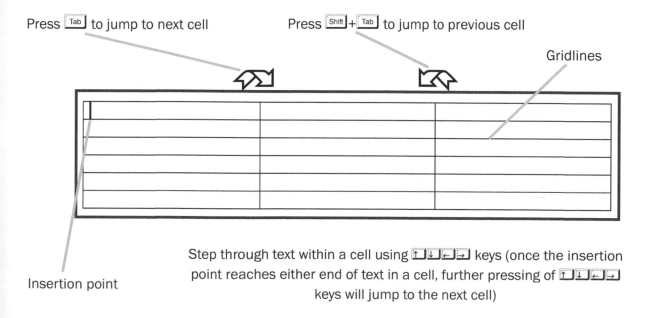

Insertion point

Step through text within a cell using `↑``↓``←``→` keys (once the insertion point reaches either end of text in a cell, further pressing of `↑``↓``←``→` keys will jump to the next cell)

Tables (cont)

Once you've created a table you can change it to suit. You can drag column widths and indents from the document ruler (bottom) and you can drag a column gridline left or right to suit directly from the table.

Tip

Whether you drag a column marker in the ruler or a table gridline, any more columns to the right of the moved element are resized proportionally — the table width doesn't change.

However, if you hold down Ctrl + Shift while you drag, the table width does change

Text wraps around and row height increases if column width isn't sufficient

Ruler is active only over active column

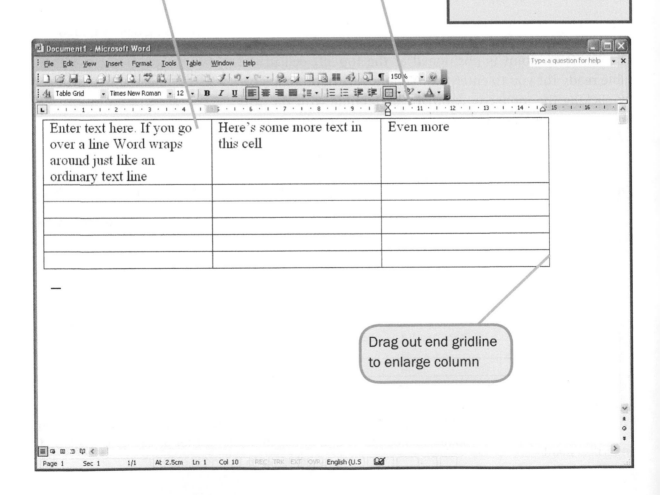

Drag out end gridline to enlarge column

Table conversions

Even if you've already entered text you can still convert it into a Word table. Simply make sure there are separators which Word recognises — commas or tabs between the items of text you want in each cell, and paragraph marks between each row — in the text.

Basic steps

1 Select the text you want to convert to a table

2 Click the Insert Table button ▦ on the Standard toolbar — that text is converted into a table

1 Select the text you want to convert into a table — make sure it has adequate separators

Capital·spending→The·Students·are·Revolting → The·Food·is·Too→Cost·(£)¶
Way·too·much → Henry→Spaghetti → 99.99¶
Way,·way·too·much → John → Eggs·and·bacon→4.50¶
Way,·way,·way·too·much→Wilhelmina → Stew → 1.38¶

Capital·spending¤	The·Students·are·Revolting¤	The·Food·is·Too¤	Cost·(£)¤
Way·too·much¤	Henry¤	Spaghetti¤	99.99¤
Way,·way·too·much¤	John¤	Eggs·and·bacon¤	4.50¤
Way,·way,·way·too·much¤	Wilhelmina¤	Stew¤	1.38¤

2 Converted into a table

Take note

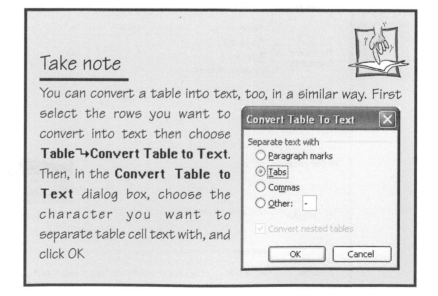

You can convert a table into text, too, in a similar way. First select the rows you want to convert into text then choose **Table� Convert Table to Text**. Then, in the **Convert Table to Text** dialog box, choose the character you want to separate table cell text with, and click OK

Graphics

You can import a graphic created in another application into a Word document. There are several kinds of graphic files you may want to import, but the principle is the same, whatever the kind. Also, once imported, any graphic can be edited in several ways.

Basic steps

- **Importing a graphic**

1 Position the insertion point where you want the graphic to be placed. Choose **Insert↪ Picture↪From File**, or type ⌈Alt⌉+⌈I⌉ then ⌈P⌉, then ⌈F⌉

2 Locate the graphic you want in the **Insert Picture** dialog box and click **OK**. The graphic is imported to your document

2 Locate graphic file you want to import

1 **Insert Picture** dialog box

Click here and choose Preview from the drop-down menu, to preview picture in box below

Resizing a graphic

■ **Editing a graphic**
1 Click a graphic in a Word document
2 Drag any of the box handles to adjust the size or shape

Once a graphic file has been imported into a Word document, editing is simple — the most basic form of editing (and the one most commonly done) is resizing to suit the document.

1 Select a graphic by clicking it

As you let go the mouse button, the graphic resizes itself

2 Drag a box handle to resize a graphic. Dragging a corner handle resizes the graphic proportionally. Dragging a middle handle resizes it disproportionately

Styles

Styles are a method of automatic formatting. They are extremely important, because:

❏ their use makes it easy to define the formats which any particular paragraph has applied to it

❏ styles are groups of formats gathered together under one label (all the formats considered in Chapter 3 — and others — can be gathered together and given just a single style name)

❏ if you apply a style to selected text all that text has the same formats applied to it simultaneously

❏ all you need to do to apply a style to selected text is choose that style from a drop-down list — the text is formatted with all the individual formats just by this one action

❏ you can use styles instantly, because any Word document has default styles already built in.

1 Enter some text into a new Word document. Don't bother applying any character or paragraph formats yet. Make sure you type in a few paragraphs and make the top paragraph and some others single line ones — say headings or subheadings

2 Select the top heading of the document (you can simply click anywhere in the first paragraph) then click the Style drop-down list box of the Formatting toolbar

2 Select the top paragraph of the entered text — you don't need to select the whole paragraph, you only need to click in it

Special resistors
There are several other types of resistors you may encounter in your electronic travels. Some of these are covered elsewhere in the book, but for completeness the main ones are listed here:
Surface mount resistors
There has always been a trend to reduce electronic devices in size. The latest step in this trend is to use miniature components that are soldered directly to a printed circuit board's copper track ie, they are mounted on the board surface (see Figure 3.12), rather than with component leads that go through the board. As such, surface mount resistors are (by their nature) extremely small, so they are not as suited to hand assembly and soldering as conventional resistors with leads. However you may find yourself working with them occasionally.
Figure 3.12 A typical surface mount resistor — colour coding or lettered markings may be used for component identification (but may not be...). Note that this is illustrated rather larger than full size — actual size is around 2 mm wide!
Thermistors
A thermistor is a resistor whose value changes according to heat. These are useful in applications that detect heat such as electronic thermometers. They vary in size and shape according to construction (they are actually made using semiconductor materials), and typical devices are shown in Figure 3.13. The symbol for a thermistor is shown in Figure 3.14.

1 Enter unformatted text into your document

3 From the Style drop-down list (a list of the default styles present in each new Word document) choose Heading 1

4 View the results of this style change

5 Repeat this for other parts of the document, choosing other headings and styles

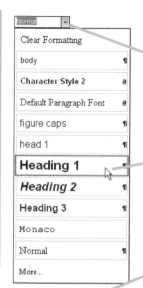

3 The Style drop-down list box. Default styles for Word documents are listed — choose Heading 1

Note how the whole paragraph has been formatted with the formats contained within the Heading 1 style — even though you only clicked in the paragragh

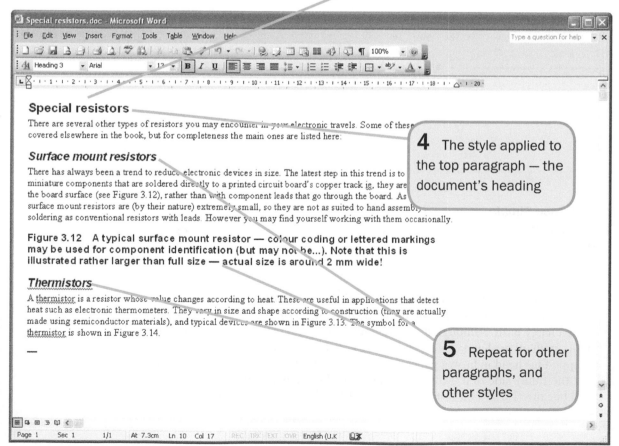

4 The style applied to the top paragraph — the document's heading

5 Repeat for other paragraphs, and other styles

Creating styles

There are three main ways you can create your own paragraph style:

❏ apply formats to your own sample text, until it is the way you want it, then create the style from those formats (for most people, this is ideal)

❏ adapt another style to suit

❏ copy styles from other documents to your own.

Basic steps

■ **Create your own**

1 To create a style from your own sample text, apply formats to your text until it is the way you want it (look again at Chapter 3 if you're a bit hazy about formatting)

2 Select the text you want to make a style of

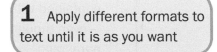

1 Apply different formats to text until it is as you want

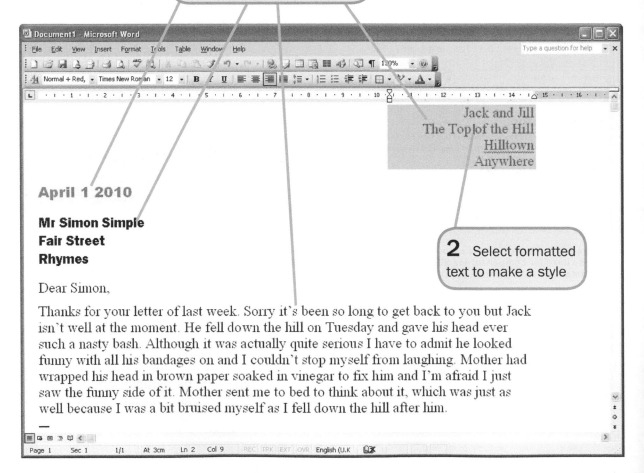

2 Select formatted text to make a style

3 Choose **Format➜Styles and Formatting**, or type [Alt]+[O] then [S], to call up the **Styles and Formatting** pane

4 Click the **New Style** button, to call up the **New Style** dialog box

5 Enter a name for your style

6 Check the **Add to template** check box, then click **OK**

If you repeat this procedure for all the different styles within your document, when you have finished you will end up with a number of styles which have been added to Word, and which will be present whenever you open a new document following that template.

Next time you want to produce a similar looking document the styles are already there to use. Simply enter your text in the new document, select the text to be formatted with any particular style, then apply the style from the Formatting toolbar's Style button drop-down list. The text is formatted as you defined.

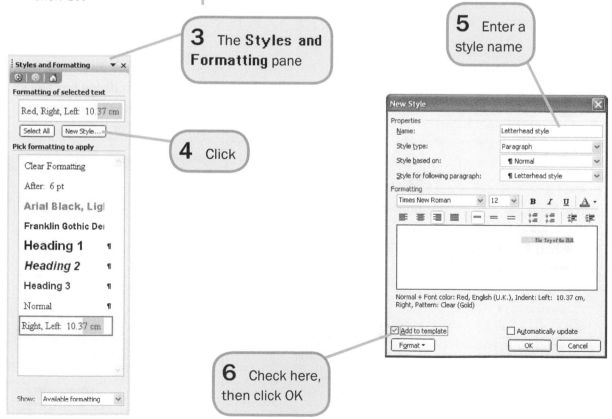

3 The **Styles and Formatting** pane

4 Click

5 Enter a style name

6 Check here, then click OK

Creating styles (cont)

One of the beauties of styles is their ability to be modified. What's more, if you modify a style all text in a document which has been formatted with that style is modified too. This is extremely useful when you're formatting a document to appear how you want it, but also it's a useful method of creating your own styles.

Basic steps

■ **Modify existing style**

1 To modify a style choose **Format⇥Styles and Formatting**, or type [Alt]+[O] then [S]

2 In the **Styles and Formatting** pane, click the drop-down button of the style you want to modify in the list, then choose **Modify** to call up the **Modify Style** dialog box

3 Click the **Format** button to drop down a list of formats which you can modify, select the format you want and in the resultant dialog box adjust formats to suit. Repeat for other formats

1 **Styles and Formatting** pane

Modify Style dialog box

2 Click the style's drop-down button, then choose **Modify**

3 Click **Format** then choose the formats you wish to modify

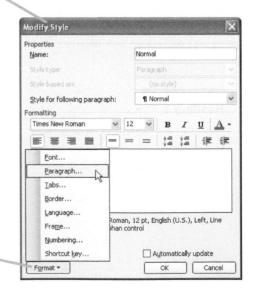

Tip

Format all text in a document with styles — that way if you want to change the document's appearance you only have to change a handful of styles, not the various text elements

Take note

When you click the Format button at step 3, you can modify any of the formats we've seen already (along with some new ones). All the formats available in the drop-down list are assigned to the style — then, when you have finished, all text which is formatted with that style is modified too. In other words, you can make some immense changes to the appearance of your document quite simply just by modifying a style

Tip

You can assign keyboard shortcuts to any style:

First, modify the style as suggested on these pages.

Next, in the Modify Style dialog box choose Shortcut key, to call up the Customize Keyboard dialog box (right). Enter the shortcut you want assigned to the style and if that shortcut isn't already used for some other function click Assign. Click Close to get back to the Modify Style dialog box, where you should then click OK.

Now you can apply a style simply by selecting the text and pressing your keyboard shortcut

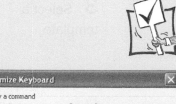

Creating styles (cont)

The last method of creating styles in a document is to copy styles from other documents which have the styles you want. It's the **Organizer** dialog box which allows you to do this, listing styles in two documents side-by-side, so that you can copy styles from one to the other.

The styles to be copied can be in a true Word document, or in a Word template. Word has many default templates which you can use for this purpose, and we'll use one to illustrate how you can do it.

- **Copying styles**
1. To copy one or more styles from one document to another, choose **Tools→Templates and Add-Ins**, or type Alt+T then I, then in the **Templates and Add-Ins** dialog box click the **Organizer** button to call up the **Organizer** dialog box

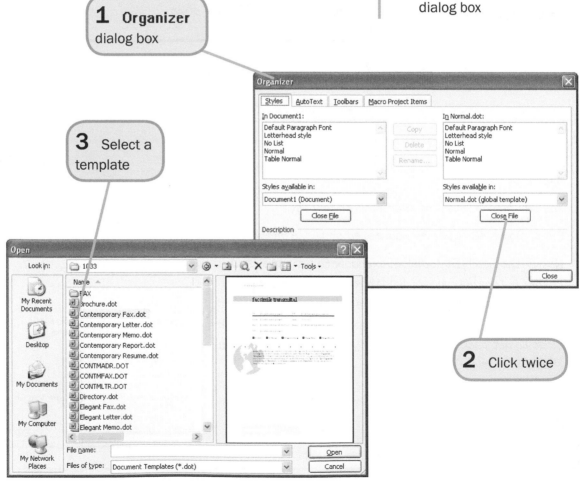

1 Organizer dialog box

3 Select a template

2 Click twice

2 Click **Close File** on the right side of the dialog box (the button changes to **Open File**) then click **Open File**. This displays a list of available files which you can select. Locate the templates folder in the MSOffice folder on your hard disk and make sure you're listing files of document template (*.dot) types

3 Select a template in the list and click **Open**. Now the **Organizer** dialog box displays all the styles in the template in a scrollable list

4 You can select individual styles, or you can select multiple styles by [Ctrl] + clicking them

5 Copy them to your own document by clicking **Copy**

6 Click **Close** to close the **Organizer** dialog box, then try out your new styles in your own document

4 Select the style or styles you want in your document

5 Once you've selected some styles, click here to copy them to your document

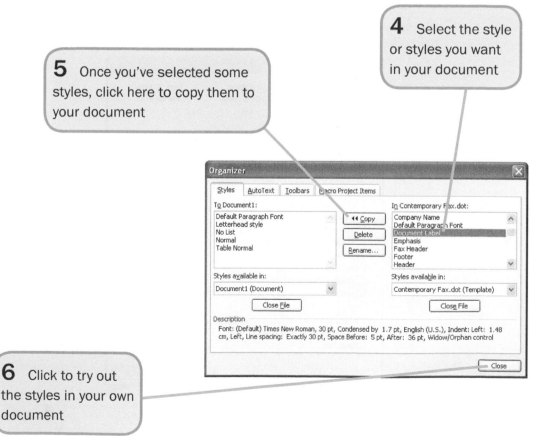

6 Click to try out the styles in your own document

109

Viewing styles in your documents

If you haven't already realized it, styles are very important to a word processor like Word. Styles form the key to producing professional documents with total consistency of formatting. Their use ensures efficient control over your documents.

You can arrange your document window to display which style is applied to a paragraph directly.

1 Choose **Tools→ Options**, or type Alt+T then O to display the **Options** dialog box

2 Click the **View** tab — if it's not already at the front of the dialog box

3 Specify a width greater than 0 in the **Style area width** box to display the style area in your document

4 Click **OK**

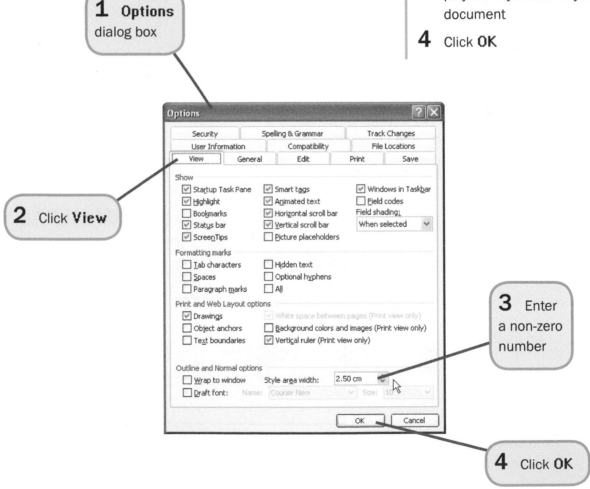

1 Options dialog box

2 Click View

3 Enter a non-zero number

4 Click OK

Your document will now display the Styles area, complete
with a listing of each paragraph's style

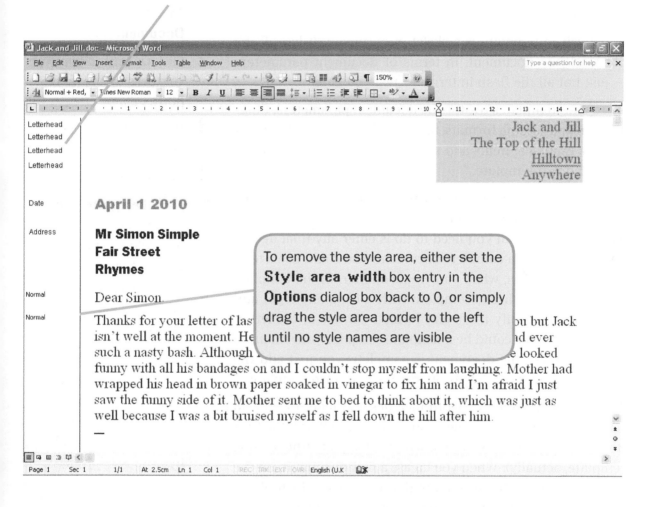

To remove the style area, either set the
Style area width box entry in the
Options dialog box back to 0, or simply
drag the style area border to the left
until no style names are visible

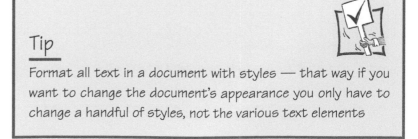

Tip

Format all text in a document with styles — that way if you
want to change the document's appearance you only have to
change a handful of styles, not the various text elements

Templates

In places in the book, the term *template* has been used, without any full explanation. Now it's time to say exactly *what* a template is.

Effectively, a template is a skeleton document. It has all the bones of any document, in terms of document parameters — just not all the flesh in terms of text you enter.

Word uses templates to store *all* document parameters. Character and paragraph formats, tables, styles, sections, AutoText entries, graphical items and so on — and even text — can all be stored in a template.

Then, when you create a new document, you can base it on the chosen template and up pops a new document looking exactly as you want it — all you need to do is enter any final details and hey, presto!, a complete document. You could use a template, for example, when you create a letter. In the template might be a letterhead, complete with a company logo, and styles which specify fonts and formats for use in the letter. Another example could be a template setup for your monthly sales figures — the document is complete; you just add the figures. See over for details of creating your own template.

A default installation of Word includes a number of built-in templates as standard. When you first startup Word, the first document on-screen is even based on a template (the Normal template, actually). When you create a new document, on the other hand, you are given an option to choose which of the built-in templates you want to use for the document.

Basic steps:

1 Choose **File→New**, or type ⎇Alt+F then N. This calls up the **New Document** pane

2 Click **On my computer**. This calls up the **Templates** dialog box

3 Click a tab to see associated templates

4 Click a template

5 Click **Template** if you want to create a new template based on the template chosen

6 Click **OK** to create the document based on that template

Tip

You can bypass the New dialog box if you want to create a document speedily. Just click the New button on the Standard toolbar and a new document — based on the Normal template — is automatically created

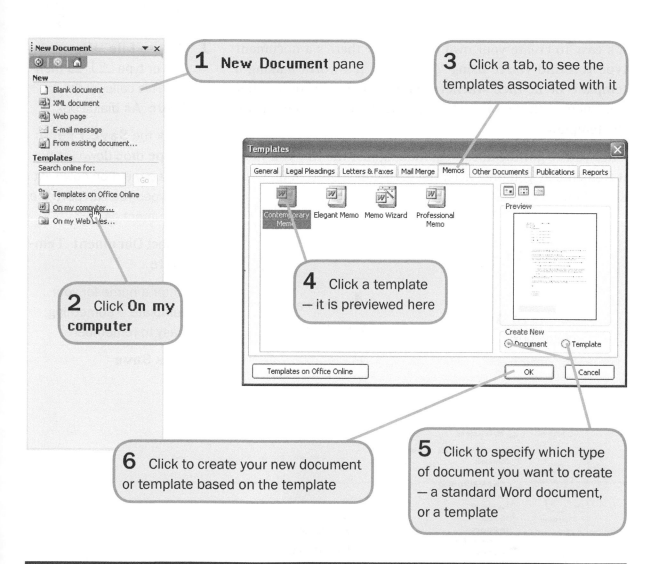

1 New Document pane

New Document

New
- Blank document
- XML document
- Web page
- E-mail message
- From existing document...

Templates
Search online for:
[ ] Go
- Templates on Office Online
- On my computer...
- On my Web Sites...

2 Click **On my computer**

Templates

General | Legal Pleadings | Letters & Faxes | Mail Merge | Memos | Other Documents | Publications | Reports

Contemporary Memo | Elegant Memo | Memo Wizard | Professional Memo

Preview

Create New
- Document
- Template

Templates on Office Online | OK | Cancel

3 Click a tab, to see the templates associated with it

4 Click a template — it is previewed here

5 Click to specify which type of document you want to create — a standard Word document, or a template

6 Click to create your new document or template based on the template

Take note

The Normal template is a special case template — it holds all the document parameters you use most in Word. All the toolbars, their buttons, their positions, the menus and shortcut keys, and everything else you have as default items, are stored in the Normal template. If you use another template to create other documents, on the other hand, all these features are still available in those other documents

Creating a template

It's easy to create your own template. If there's a document type you find you're using quite a lot, it's worth making a template of it, then whenever you want to create another document with the same style just create the document from the template.

Once you've got the document looking just the way you want it (remember, you only need the bare bones of it), follow the steps here.

Basic steps:

1 Choose **File→Save As**, or type `Alt`+`F` then `A`. This calls up the **Save As** dialog box

2 Click the **Save File as Type** drop-down list box to see the drop-down list of types you can save the document as

3 Select **Document Template**

4 Enter a name for your template — something easy to remember

5 Click **Save**

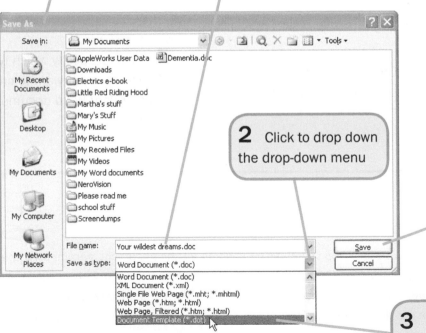

1 **Save As** dialog box

4 Enter a name you'll remember

2 Click to drop down the drop-down menu

5 Click to save template

3 Click the **Document Template** option

Here's an example of a template for a letterhead. It combines a heading with a border (the underlining) and a simple graphic

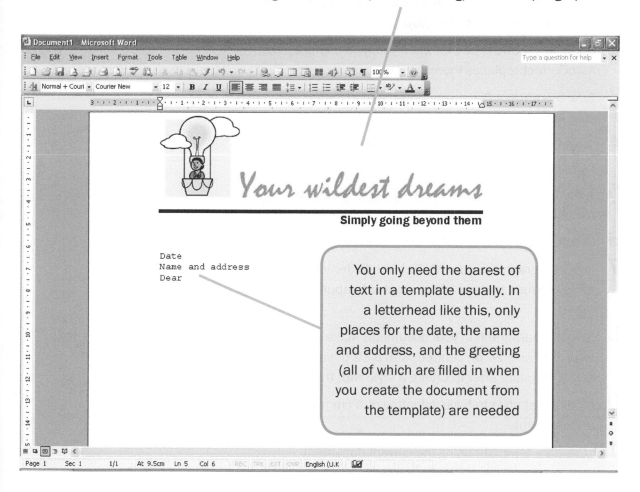

You only need the barest of text in a template usually. In a letterhead like this, only places for the date, the name and address, and the greeting (all of which are filled in when you create the document from the template) are needed

Tip

You can modify any of the existing built-in templates, too. This can be a good way to get started with templates in Word, because most of what you need is already there.

Simply adapt the existing template to suit your requirements, then choose File ⮡Save As or type Alt + F then A, as before, and give it a new name

Exercises

1 In a new blank document, type several sentences and paragraphs of text. Find and replace all instances of the word *the*, with the word *eggcup*

2 Setup AutoCorrect so that when you type the letters *ec*, AutoCorrect replaces them with the word *eggcup*

3 Type the phrase *Place your boiled egg in the ec*, and make sure AutoCorrect is working

4 Select the sentence *Place your boiled egg in the eggcup*, and create an AutoText entry for it, with the entry name *pec*

5 Type the phrase *England expects every man to pec*, to make sure AutoText is working

6 Create a four column table with three rows

7 Import a graphic in your My Pictures folder into a cell of the table. Reduce the size of the graphic to approximately 3 cm high

8 Select a paragraph in your document. Make the font colour blue, font size 24 pt, centred, with a 12 pt space before and 8 pt space after it. Create a style with that formatting

9 Modify that style to have indenting of 4 cm from the left and the right

10 Create a template using the current document

Index

P

Page layout view 73
Painting a format 50
Paragraph
  formats 52
  formatting 44
  styles 44
Paragraph dialog box
  indenting 55
Paragraph formats 52
  indenting 54
Paragraph formatting 44

R

Replacing
  formats 88
  text 88
Ruler
  indent stops 54

S

Saving 16
ScreenTips 6
Section 68
  end 68
  formatting 68
Selecting text 30

Setting up a document 70
Shading 60
Spelling
  checking 90
  spelling button 90
  underline highlighting 90
Status bar 3, 27
Styles 102
  copying 108
  creating 104, 106
  modifying 106
Symbols 40

T

Table menu 5
Tables 96
  converting into text 99
  converting text into 99
  creating from toolbar 97
  dragging boundaries 98
  dragging gridlines 98
  moving around 97
Tabs 58
Templates 20, 112
Text
  editing 28
  selecting 30
Text flow
  orphan 56
  widow 56